ROACH RHINO REDUX

An aging thesis writer asks:
"What hath half a century wrought?"

ROACH RHINO REDUX

REVISITING PARALLELS
IN KAFKA AND IONESCO

FIFTIETH ANNIVERSARY EDITION
featuring updated research by the author,
plus a look at the plight of endangered rhinos

ETHAN HIRSH

Green Mountain Farm Press
Lincoln, Missouri

www.g-m-f.press

© 2019 Ethan Hirsh

First Edition
Printed in the United States of America

Cover and book design by Claire Crevey

ISBN 978-0-9997402-2-4
Ebook ISBN 978-0-9997402-3-1
10 9 8 7 6 5 4 3 2 1

This book is dedicated to
the rangers who have bravely chosen
to serve as guardians and protectors
of rhinos in the wild.

CONTENTS

FOR THE UNINITIATED

Most of us learned at a fairly early age that "metamorphosis" refers to the miraculous maturation cycle through which caterpillars form a chrysalis and reemerge as butterflies, a process captured countless times in time-lapse nature films and videos. Many other insects go through similar stages. In literature, the theme of transformation has shown up for at least the last two millennia, such as in Ovid's collection of mythological Latin poetry called *Metamorphoses.*

My 1967 thesis examined how two writers applied the device of metamorphosis or transformative change in different ways to achieve similar literary and dramatic goals. In case you are unfamiliar with the two works discussed in this volume, here are back-of-a-business-card versions (okay, large-cocktail-napkin) to help you make sense of this study.

> Franz Kafka's short story/novella *The Metamorphosis* opens with traveling salesman Gregor Samsa figuring out while still in bed that he's been transformed overnight into a super-sized bug. The rest of the story deals with the anguish this new state of being brings both him and his family—parents, sister and housekeeper. He dies at the end, a victim of the repulsion they can no longer resist.
>
> In his play *Rhinoceros,* Eugène Ionesco uses the opposite tack to arrive at individual despair and isolation, having every character but one leave humanhood behind to become a

thick-skinned pachyderm. In the end, Bérenger is left utterly alone in his determination to resist joining the mob of rampaging rhinos, Ionesco's metaphor for the lack of resistance when Nazis invaded France, a scene he witnessed personally in 1940.

QUESTIONS, QUESTIONS

"Why did you do it?" they ask. Acquaintances hearing of my thesis resuscitation project for the first time usually exhibit a demeanor only slightly less abrupt than a local newsperson might show while accosting a freshly arrested axe murderer.

I'm always very understanding. After all, how many people do you know who have not only taken their old thesis off the shelf and reread it, but have then gone on to renew their research and publish an update? None? Same here!

What, other than self-admiration, could motivate such an uncalled-for and gratuitous undertaking? During the arduous reformatting and eventual reintroduction of this work, I kept asking myself that very question. What was the insistent draw I kept feeling—for decades—until in 2017 it became impossible to resist?

As I lay on my back at night, flailing my insect-like arms in the dark, I pondered Gregor Samsa's hold on my imagination. Ambulating midday city streets, I tried to wrap my mind around Ionesco's pertinacious relevance in today's world, with so much ugly history about to be repeated by those ignoring its proverbial lessons.

I barely escaped untrampled when, seemingly out of nowhere, a full-blown rhinoceros thundered across the median, toppling a silver-toned light pole between a bike rack and a parked minivan. (I swear, it was sporting a red baseball cap, too.)

Yes, I concluded, there *would* be plenty of fodder to entice me back to my lofty but practically prehistoric undergraduate role of apprentice-level literary critic.

Later, safely back at my desk, I would read another chapter from my 1967 opus, and find it quite (I'm unembarrassed to say) entertaining—not just recalling the caveman-era pounding I gave my military-grade Remington portable typewriter (more a cross between a percussion instrument and a boat anchor than a piece of office equipment), but also the joy and delight I felt while writing about two such absurd and rightfully famous masterworks. I relived that feeling I had at 20 years of age, not just being scholarly and analytical but drafting a creative vocabulary to reflect the uniqueness of the two specimens I was putting under the scope.

I remember the effort as two semesters of hard work, but I equally remember that doing the thesis was a lot of fun.

The challenge I eventually lay before my own no-longer-flailing feet was two-fold: (1) Find a broader audience for my original thesis, which resides in its as-filed form in the Special Collections section of the M. D. Anderson Library at the University of Houston's Central Campus; and (2), satisfy my curiosity about what's been going on with Kafka's *The Metamorphosis* and Ionesco's *Rhinoceros* since 1967.

Is there anything out there in the worlds of literature and drama that would alter or reinforce the validity of my findings? Are the two works collecting dust or still being read and produced? Has anything *changed* about their place in the world's exponentially overladen consciousness? In short, how are they handling that "passage of time" thing?

As so often happens in this Google-centric era, the more I looked, the more I found data I didn't even know I was searching for. As the momentum, along with the used space on my hard drive, kept building, my findings percolated and finally jelled. It's now my pleasure to share them with you in a streamlined form and non-adjudicated environment.

For the typical scholarly criticism in academic journals of the 1960s this would be way too personal a statement, but I'll say it anyway: I *love* these two works! I can come back to each of them for a reunion, as with a favorite symphony. I've thought of them frequently over the past five decades. I still have them on my nearest bookshelf, and I visualize some of their scenes from time to time. That may be partly due to my affinity for the bizarre and absurd, but it's also because I identify empathically with characters in stories and plays, especially ones as memorable as these two.

How could I *not* be caught up forever by Kafka's opening sentence in *Metamorphosis,* one of the most studied, effective and (in the original German) ambiguous first lines in any short story ever. "As Gregor Samsa awoke one morning from uneasy dreams he found himself transformed in his bed into a gigantic insect." He soon confirms: "It was no dream."[1] Likewise, by Bérenger's final solo in *Rhinoceros:* "People who try to hang on to their individuality always come to a bad end!" Yet, he declares in the play's closing words, "I'm not capitulating!"[2]

Notably, those are the most frequently quoted lines—Kafka's first sentence and Ionesco's last. As my 1967 thesis demonstrated, these two pieces of literature are in some ways opposites while managing to achieve similar effects.

The chronometer has turned past the 50-year mark since getting my undergraduate degree and I'm still looking at both works in the rearview mirror. They resonate with me today, more than ever. I had already pretty well talked myself into proceeding with this semi-centennial thesis update project as I neared the end of a complete rereading of my original work. Then suddenly, in the "Closing Statement" in Chapter IV, I slammed smack into this sentence:

> In the light of Ionesco's remarks [regarding how any writer's works will be viewed in the future within the context of all literary history], **this study should be remade in twenty-five, perhaps fifty, years from now.** [Emphasis added.]

Holy crapoli! *I said that??!!* There it was, looming startlingly in plain sight before me like Arthur C. Clarke's giant interplanetary monolith

1 Franz Kafka, "The Metamorphosis," *Selected Short Stories of Franz Kafka,* edited and translated by Edwin and Willa Muir (Random House, Inc., 1952), page 19.

2 Eugène Ionesco, "Rhinoceros," *Rhinoceros and Other Plays,* translated by Derek Prouse (Grove Press, Inc., 1960), page 107.

reborn in Kubrick's *2001: A Space Odyssey*—my long-buried call to action. I had intentionally implanted it to encourage new generations of scholars to keep taking close looks at these two authors periodically and share their findings with the world. To ensure the process gets rolling, I'm herewith giving it my own little half-a-century shove.

Every so often, I had worried about the durability of *Metamorphosis* and *Rhinoceros*, but both seem to have survived the latter half of the Twentieth Century and early part of the Twenty-first quite well.

In Kafka's case, the themes of alienation in the corporate-industrial environment and selective persecution within nations and families remain relevant, visible and talked about. Meanwhile, with the stimuli of increasingly diverse media and performing artist crossovers, today's experience of established works ventures into new and ever more varied channels. I found Kafka's *Metamorphosis* not only in print, but in audio performance, multiple films and videos, musical compositions, modern dance choreography, opera, and even a graphic novel.

Unlike Kafka, who died in 1924, Ionesco was still actively writing in 1967 and he continued his dramatic output through 1980. I'm sure I underappreciated his contemporariness when I was a student in the '60s. While his works have not been reversioned as extensively as Kafka's, he has not been forgotten, and for reasons made clear in the exhibits, *Rhinoceros* in particular has undergone a significant revival in just the last few years.

It is probably no surprise to you that many productions of both Kafka and Ionesco can be viewed instantly on YouTube. I tried not to be distracted during my Internet searches by the "adorable baby rhino" videos, which are indeed easy to come by. (I gave up after counting the first 200!) They're posted by zoos and zoo visitors, wildlife rescuers and owners of pet rhinos (not usually apartment dwellers), all eager to show how smart and playful the frolicking little beasts are as they protect Mama Rhino, or play well with other species, or enjoy their first shower, or test the upper limits of the pachydermal performance envelope.

There are also sites, of course, that play up the opposite end of the rhinocerene persona—the sheer immensity, the poor vision, the thundering speed, the destructiveness, and unfortunately, the sad place of despair that wearing such a formidable and coveted horn leaves those beasts which remain.

One by one, their species are disappearing forever, victims of an insane black market. The planet's last male northern white rhino, an infirm 45-year-old named Sudan, was euthanized by his veterinarians in Kenya in March 2018.

Rhino species go back between 10 and 20 million years, which makes them a very modern development compared to the cockroach, which has been around for 200 to 300 million! All 4,500 roach species continue to thrive around the world and a handful of those species manage to be quite good at terrorizing their human cohabitants.

Roaches have their share of online videos, but only a very few are labeled "adorable." Most are about methods of extermination, the control of invasive species, expressions of disgust, cockroach milk (the newest superfood), bread from cockroach flour (yet another superfood), and the occasional pseudo-art piece such as the one about a Philippine man who designed a miniature electric chair for carrying out capital punishment of imprisoned roaches (presumably reserved for those duly convicted of the most egregious infractions).

Other sites take you to cockroach-themed video games, and even a neuroscience-based cellphone app that makes it possible to manipulate a roach's navigational choices through an electronic chip mounted on the insect's back. (Think how useful this could be to a tenth-grade student wanting to steer a creeps-inducing cockroach toward the desk of an unsuspecting schoolmate or teacher.)

You obviously won't have much luck finding a Cockroach Conservancy, or a Disney-Pixar animated musical blockbuster called *The Roach King*. Other than the EPA's control of hazardous pesticides there aren't exactly a ton of laws, regulations, organizations, movements or protest marches to protect the loathed and lowly cucaracha.

The question going begging here is, what does all that tell us in terms of literary criticism, particularly in the context of this thesis? *Next to nothing*, except that in spite of their differences, both of the creatures selected by our two authors effectively capture human attention in distinctive and potent ways.

Of course, the German term "Ungeziefer" penned by Kafka to denote Gregor's post-transformational form ("vermin" in English) does not literally *mean* "cockroach," or even "insect." Yet, some version of roach-like critter is what typically pops into the mind of the average American reader, thanks to several popular translations of *Metamorphosis* that make the choice for us, even though a "vermin" could be anything from a louse to a weasel (or, as used in the nastiest sociopolitical context, even an undesirable human).

In English, "vermin" is not species-specific but by definition implies a creature that is harmful, hard to control, offensive … and usually small. A vermin that is monstrous, then, is unnatural and especially stomach-churning. Kafka's descriptor "ungeheueres," which translates to "tremendous" or "monstrous," takes care of the size issue (sorry, lice), while his depiction of Gregor's various repugnant physical traits decidedly steers one's imagination roachward. Most likely he is hideous, abnormal, freakish and mutant, and therefore especially disturbing for his family members to face. Gregor has indeed woken to a nightmarish situation.

There are a number of worthy translations of *Metamorphosis* today, among them eight that could be considered prominent. It would be interesting to devote a whole thesis to comparing them to one another. However, it's unlikely that any of their variations would cause me to alter the observations I made 50 years ago.

Out of curiosity, I tested how Google Translate would do Kafka's opening sentence. Here's what the app gave me nearly instantaneously: "One morning, when Gregor Samsa awoke from troubled dreams, he found himself transformed into a tremendous vermin in his bed." Not bad, and literally correct (though for greater effect I would have placed "into a tremendous vermin" at the end of the sentence).

I've devoted a lot of discussion here to a single linguistic issue in *Metamorphosis,* the one raised by Kafka's very first sentence. Why? Many of the exhibits of my findings show a presumption that Gregor turned into a cockroach even though various translators have used the general "vermin" (Kafka's choice) or the still somewhat general "insect," while others specify "cockroach," "beetle" or even "dung beetle." Had he wished, Kafka could have used one of the several specific German terms for cockroach. Gregor could have wakened as a Kakerlake or a Küchenschabe, for example. But the ill-defined and mysterious "Ungeziefer" sounds so much more ominous!

Since Ionesco's use of the term "rhinoceros" is very straightforward and not subject to misinterpretation, I found no reason for a parallel discussion of French-to-English translation in the context of species. At one point in *Rhinoceros,* characters debate whether a rhino that whizzed past had one horn or two, was Asian or African.

In a great demonstration of absurdity, the argument goes on for nearly 9 percent of the script and its dialog becomes hysterical in both senses of the word. How Ionesque! At one point a "professional logician" introduced to Bérenger says "you have got away from the problem which instigated the debate." (*Rhinoceros,* pages 34–35.) Yet he, too, traipses down an irrelevant path. The point Ionesco makes is, don't get distracted by the minutiae of an immense problem. If I may quote my 1967 self, "It is by no means essential to the understanding of the story."

Nor is the quibble about whether Gregor was a cockroach, or even an insect. The situation established in the opening sentence would for him be just as horrendous, and the outcome just as fatal, no matter to which phylum and species he might be classified by a consulting zoologist.

I find it interesting that Kafka was Czech but wrote in German, and Ionesco was Romanian and wrote in French. Did these linguistic twists have any bearing on the style or success of either author? I also wonder how translators into languages other than English have dealt with the "Ungeziefer" issue. I would love to know how their foreign-language interpretations of the famous first sentence read when rendered into English.

Toward the end of this project, I began to wonder why I kept finding more discussion and revamping of *Metamorphosis* than of *Rhinoceros.* I finally reasoned that it was due to the inherent difference between a story and a play. Kafka's writing is a force to be reckoned with. Ionesco's drama is more about situational action and staging—memorable scenes rather than memorable phrases. Hence, the 100 years of scholarly study into Kafka's exact wording and meaning, and the plethora of variations and modifications on the theme of Gregor's transformation. Meanwhile, *Rhinoceros* lives on around the world through theatrical productions in which directors adapt the script, set and props to their venue, capabilities and audience, but keep Ionesco's dramatic core intact.

This aspect of comparing the two works was never a focus of my original thesis. It only became apparent after reviewing their evolution over the past half century.

I turned 20 as the first of my two semesters of thesis writing came to a close. Here and there I can see my phrasing and word choice would be slightly different today, but I've left the original text (provided later in this volume) entirely as it first appeared, other than to scan the typewritten document and reformat it for appearance and readability. I'm satisfied that both works' continued popularity confirms the rightness of my choice of topic.

Who would have guessed in the 1960s, only two decades after the end of World War II, that 50 years later fascist tendencies would again be rearing their head on both sides of the Atlantic; that neo-Nazis would frequently make the nightly news in America; or that electronic social media would be provoking novel stampedes and hysteria of various types more or less daily.

Again, as I wrote in 1967, this study should be remade in another 25 or 50 years. If you're a budding literary critic, here's a project to revisit when you're in your 40s, or 70s—or both. In the interests of uneasy-dreams analysis and corralling rampant rhinoism in all its forms, let's keep the process going.

If you're up for it, mark your to-do lists for 2042 and 2067 *now,* before leaving this page!

EXHIBITS

To answer my question "What hath half a century wrought?" I searched the Internet for mentions of *Metamorphosis* and *Rhinoceros* and compiled a chronological list of what I found in the way of books, films, stage productions and other events post-1967. The list is by no means complete, but represents instead a quick and somewhat serendipitous survey of what's taken place in the ongoing lives of both works.

The good news is, it's quite a lot! To discuss it all in detail would make this revisitation far longer than the original thesis, so instead my list merely provides boiled-down driblets of research, with references in a separate webliography so any eager scholar can pick up one or more leads and run with them.

So—the list, please!

METAMORPHOSIS

EXHIBIT M-1 ▸ 1969/1989

Steven Berkoff's radical adaptation of Kafka's story for the stage premieres at London's Roundhouse with the adaptor-director himself in the lead role. The six characters mime and shout in a stark setting, with Gregor writhing around in an elevated jungle gym-like room made of metal scaffolding. Over time the play gains international acceptance (Czech Republic and Japan, for example), with Gregor played by such diverse stars as Tim Roth, Roman Polanski and Mikhail Baryshnikov.

Two decades after the premiere, *New York Times* critic Frank Rich finds it very difficult to find anything nice to say about the show's 1989 Broadway run, taking particular issue with what he perceives as ideological distortions of Kafka's themes and mostly poor use of Baryshnikov's talents.

EXHIBIT M-2 ▸ 1975

Czech writer-director Jan Nemec heads the West German production of *Die Verwandlung*, a 55-minute TV movie of his adaptation of *The Metamorphosis*. The story is told from Gregor's perspective but without ever showing his verminous appearance. You can view the whole thing on YouTube in German with Turkish(!) subtitles. More than one German-speaking YouTube viewer applies the Deutsch s-word to describe what he finds.

Nemec, once one of his native land's New Wave directors, does not hide his discomfort: "I just do not fit in in Germany.... When I filmed the Kafka story which was made as a slapstick, a German critic wrote that it was incomprehensible how a Czechoslovak film director could make fun of classics from German literature." Nemec is one of several New Wavers, including Miloš Forman, who fled when the Soviets invaded in 1968 to crush the short-lived Prague Spring and its attempt at cultural openness. Unlike Forman's, his career never recovers.

EXHIBIT M-3 ▸ 1976

Writer-director Ivo Dvorák adapts Kafka's story for his Swedish-language movie *Förvandlingen*, a black-and-white and color 35mm production of the Swedish Film Institute. The 88-minute work is nominated for Best Feature at the 1976 Chicago International Film Festival. Though sometimes working in Sweden, Dvorák is a native of Prague. AllMovie gives his feature only two out of five stars.

EXHIBIT M-4 ▸ 1978

Ten minutes is all it takes for writer-director Caroline Leaf to tell Gregor's tale in *The Metamorphosis of Mr. Samsa,* a darkly animated short. Perhaps that's because her medium is beach sand on a sheet of glass. Produced by the American Film Institute, the National Film Board of Canada and The National Endowment for the Arts, the film opens in Poland in 1978 and reaches many other foreign audiences more than 25 years later. At least it's still about Gregor Samsa and his predicament.

Many other movies appear over the decades with the title of "Metamorphosis," spanning the spectrum of the cult-horror genre—a mad scientist messing with his own DNA; space aliens hell-bent on destruction of Earthlings; zombies trying the Occupy protocol; you name it....

EXHIBIT M-5 ▸ 1983

With an English libretto by Steven Berkoff (see Exhibit M-1), Graham Cox conducts Victoria State Opera's world premiere of *Metamorphosis,* which is now a 100-minute chamber opera in six scenes, in Melbourne. Composer Brian Howard scores six singers and 12 musicians on strings, select winds, electric guitar and an array of percussion. Combining that with a Berkoff-style multi-level set made of scaffolding, the production amplifies the dark side of Kafka's tale. The opera goes on to be staged by other companies in Sydney, Perth and, with choreography added, Lismore.

EXHIBIT M-6 ▸ 1988

Minimalist composer Philip Glass writes five short piano pieces, five to seven minutes each, titled *Metamorphosis One, Metamorphosis Two* and so on. All are included in his album Solo Piano released the following year. The compositions are inspired by Kafka's story of transformation, and *Three* and *Four* are used as incidental music for theatrical versions of the tale. *One* and *Two* eventually are heard in various films (notably, *The Hours*) and television shows (including *Battlestar Galactica*). Several other pianists record all five, and *One* is picked up by the rock band Pearl Jam as their concert overture.

After writing an opera based on Kafka's *In the Penal Colony,* in 2010 Glass tells *The Telegraph's* Ivan Hewett, "I've been reading Kafka seriously since I was 15. For a young person, the sense of strangeness and the bizarre is very attractive. There's a sort of authenticity about it." His second Kafka opera, *The Trial,* premieres in Wales in 2014.

EXHIBIT M-7 ▸ 2000

Bongo Comics issues its sixth annual Halloween-season volume of *Bart Simpson's Treehouse of Horror,* titled *Spine-Tingling Spooktacular.* It includes a Kafka parody by guest writer Peter Kuper, internationally known illustrator and comics creator, called *Metamorph Simpsons.* Homer has a new buggish body and the family tries to cope.

Two years later, an episode of *The Simpsons* introduces Café Kafka, a coffeehouse for the college crowd in the family's hometown of Springfield. Exterior signage features a large cockroach above the sidewalk, while interior walls are hung with posters of famous roaches. In 2017 the café becomes a premium property in the online video game The Simpsons—Tapped Out.

EXHIBIT M-8 ▸ 2002

Blue Hen/Putnam publishes *Insect Dreams: The Half Life of Gregor Samsa,* a 480-page surreal novel by American author and activist Marc Estrin conceived shortly after his 1998 visit to Kafka's grave in Prague. Barely surviving his family-inflicted death-by-apple, Gregor finds himself on a mission to save mankind from itself, visiting with dozens of famous figures from the arts and sciences, activist movements and government in such places as Vienna, New York, Los Alamos, Washington, and even a Japanese internment camp.

The *Christian Science Monitor* calls the book a "new cult classic" while *SFGate,* online child of the *San Francisco Chronicle,* calls it "ambitious and arresting" and names it one of the 100 best books of the year.

EXHIBIT M-9 ▸ 2003

The Metamorphosis wakes from uneasy dreams to find itself turned into an 80-page hardback graphic novel (Crown) by Peter Kuper, the artist-adaptor who did the Simpsons horror comic two years earlier (see Exhibit M-7). Crown's Penguin Random House, which issues the paperback a year later, says Kuper is deftly able to "merge American cartooning with German expressionism" and bring the tale to life in new ways.

EXHIBIT M-10 ▸ 2006

In a startling reverse twist, *Metamorphosis* goes completely noir with William Lashner's highly original, mirror-image novel *Kockroach,* in which the title character wakes to find he has left the species for which he is named and turned into a human! The rest of the 356-page book, published under the pen name Tyler Knox by William Morrow and Company/Harper Collins, follows the transformee as he adapts to the various demands of manly existence in the canyons of New York City. Both he and the reader discover the many ways roachly character fits right in with human business, politics, crime and love. Published translations include Italian and Portuguese.

EXHIBIT M-11 ▸ 2008

With the one and only Benedict Cumberbatch at the mike, Kafka's story comes exponentially more alive than ever on BBC Radio 7 (now 4). The BBC re-airs all four episodes of the popular series more or less annually for the next decade and eventually issues it as an audiobook and CD. *WARNING!* Exposure to the audio of this particular reading of Kafka's famed opening sentence, while non-caloric, can be seriously addictive. Be prepared to listen to all 98 minutes uninterrupted.

EXHIBIT M-12 ▸ 2010

A remote-control robotic camera with a spherical lens gives audiences a truly vermin-eyed view of Gregor Samsa's waking nightmare in the 40-minute film *Metamorphosis: Immersive Kafka,* shot in Budapest by director Sándor Kardos. It's named Best Short Film in the 2011 Hollywood Reel Independent Film Festival. Using the PanoCAST system, the brilliant techies behind the production, from Hungary and Los Angeles, go on to add DVD-based and online immersive interactive experiences that allow the viewer to control camera angle and access other features. Their cockroach-level roving shooter is like a cross between a Roomba® Robot Vacuum and Google's Street View camera car.

Despite the wildly effective camera angles, which Kafka allegedly would have liked (the filmmakers cite his diaries), many viewers remain incensed by the film's radically altered ending.

EXHIBIT M-13 ▸ 2011/2013

At Linbury Studio Theatre in London, the Royal Opera House premieres Arthur Pita's *Metamorphosis*. A year earlier he took a volume of Kafka stories on a vacation to Jamaica and imagined a production starring Royal Ballet's principal dancer Edward Watson. The production repeats in 2012 in London and is filmed for broadcast and DVD, then hits New York in 2013. The choreography and performance receive lavish praise, with Watson's own metamorphosis to become verminized Gregor called "an exceptional embodiment of a living nightmare" (ballet.co.uk) and a "physical tour de force" that "sees the sinewy, hyperflexible Watson twisted into anguished and inhumanly weird shapes" (*The Observer*).

EXHIBIT M-14 ▸ 2012/2016

British filmmaker Chris Swanton releases his movie adaptation of *Metamorphosis* at the Montreal World Film Festival, billing it as the first full-length English-language version to hit the screen. Four years later, his offering expands with the Centenary Edition, featuring a companion book with a new translation of the novella, commentary and a study guide, as well as a *Behind the Scenes* short showing the director's formidable technical and interpretive challenges. At 85 minutes, the reworked film is about 15 minutes shorter but adds opening music, a narrator, enhanced computer-generated insect imagery, and harder-to-understand bug-speak to bring out Gregor's difficulty communicating—but with subtitles.

EXHIBIT M~15 ▸ 2013

On July 3, his 130th birthday, Franz Kafka subtly reaches his biggest audience *EVER* via Google's home page doodle, seen by searcher-surfers worldwide in the course of their **three-and-a-quarter billion** Google searches in a single day. Paying homage to *The Metamorphosis,* the search engine's name appears in illustrated all-caps sprouting spiky insect legs while Gregor marches through a doorway standing in for the "O." He's apparently midway through his transformation, walking upright with briefcase, hat and tie but sporting a roach-like body. Foretelling his end, the fatal apple rests atop the foot of the "L."

EXHIBIT M~16 ▸ 2013

In its October 28 issue, *The New Yorker* publishes *Samsa in Love,* a story by best-selling Japanese author Haruki Murakami. The work appears again in 2017 in Murakami's seven-story collection *Men Without Women* (228 pages, Alfred A. Knopf). The story opens with some person, or unspecified creature, waking up in Gregor Samsa's bed and somehow knowing that he has indeed become, or perhaps mysteriously returned to being, Gregor. Vagueness runs deep in this story. The transformed, or de-transformed, Gregor inexplicably knows some things, or seems to, but finds other things unknowable. In fact, thinking for him is too burdensome altogether, and hunger causes extreme pain. Home alone, he has a lot to figure out!

His puzzlement continues when a female hunchback locksmith makes a service call to the Samsa residence. Even though he's made only partial progress learning how to use his new two-legged body, Gregor finds the deformed woman's femaleness attractive, then arous-ing, leading him to conclude that being human might not be so bad after all. The tale ends as he decides to meet life head-on. He resolves to "return to the second floor and figure out the proper way to dress."

From a literal standpoint, very little happens and very little is explained. Metaphorically, the new Gregor is getting a new chance at life, at overcoming alienation, and establishing meaningful human contact. Writing in the *Chicago Tribune,* Shoshana Olidort sees *Samsa in Love* as "yet another iteration of a motif … in which unrestricted male lust is glorified under the guise of existential loneliness and female characters serve as mere vehicles for the fulfillment or denial of male longing." Is she overreacting? In an interview, Murakami says his aim with the volume of stories is to convey "isolation, and what it means emotionally."

His acclaimed 2002 novel *Kafka on the Shore,* released in English in 2005, has a 15-year-old lead character who adopts the name Kafka to honor the Czech writer. The book is a work of magical realism rife with intertwining riddles. Perhaps this is a clue that Murakami inhabits a complex and surreal world very different from ours, in which case his writing must be viewed through a suitably irregular lens.

EXHIBIT M-17 ▸ 2014

A year-and-a-half ahead of the centennial of Kafka's German original, W. W. Norton & Company publishes Susan Bernofsky's new translation of *The Metamorphosis.* In the included afterword, she comments on the complicated and consequential nature of the translator's art. Norton's website says Bernofsky "strives to capture both the humor and the humanity in this macabre tale, underscoring the ways in which Gregor Samsa's grotesque metamorphosis is just the physical manifestation of his longstanding spiritual impoverishment."

Other new English translations appear the same year, including by Christopher Moncrieff (Alma Classics) and John R. Williams (Wordsworth Classics). The Williams version is "highly recommended" by *The Guardian's* WB Gooderham.

EXHIBIT M-18 ▸ 2014/2017

In perhaps the greatest Kafka tribute of all time, while at the Lucca Film Festival in Italy to accept a Lifetime Achievement Award, David ("Twin Peaks") Lynch says he's giving up the idea of doing a *Metamorphosis* adaptation, citing more than just cost or technical challenges.

Continuing the conversation three years later, he tells fans at the 2017 Rome Film Festival that after drafting a whole script, he realized he could never improve on Kafka's original. "That story is so full of words that, when I was finished writing, I realized it was better on paper than it could ever be on film."

And the Oscar for Restraint, Good Sense and Literary Appreciation goes to....

EXHIBIT M-19 ▸ 2015

Celebrating the story's centennial, BBC Radio devotes a week-long series entitled "In the Shadow of Kafka" to examine *The Metamorphosis* every which way and sideways, with supplemental pieces published in *The Independent* and various blogs. Analysts compare translations, particularly the endlessly debated choice of species (or non-species) and whether it was Kafka's intent to be ambiguous or merely the nature of the German language that caused this fog.

They also trace cultural and political themes; wonder how consciously Kafka foretold the genocide to come; and label themes and passages autobiographical or universal, or both. It's a crash course in Metamorphosology.

EXHIBIT M-20 ▸ 2015

Writer-director Igor Plischke releases his half-hour German-language short at the Hof International Film Festival in Bavaria. The loosely adapted screenplay places Gregor Samsa in modern times as he crumbles with a mental breakdown after becoming overwhelmed by his slick corporate job in Berlin's textile industry. The movie is a co-production of POISON GmbH and Bavarian Radio Television.

EXHIBIT M-21 ▸ 2016

Mito Studio, an "incubating environment and playground" attached to the Budapest-based Mito digital agency, launches Metamorphosis: The Game. Players navigate you-know-who safely to his bed by typing in words from the story's text. Correctly entered words "become solid platforms on which Gregor Samsa, our hero, can crawl," says Mito's website. You can also keep Gregor safe by preventing him from going the wrong direction or suffering a fatal fall.

The Hungarian whiz kid developers are Máté Cziner, Máté Roskó, Csongor Jónás and Szabolcs Endrödy.

EXHIBIT M-22 ▸ 2018

Opera Australia stages a revival of the Berkoff-based opera (see Exhibit M-5) in September at its scenery workshop in Sydney, which writer Jo Litson calls "the perfect, grungy setting for the dark, challenging chamber opera." In October the production moves to Melbourne, where the work premiered 35 years earlier with Lyndon Terracini cast as Gregor. Now Artistic Director, Terracini gets to welcome the audience at curtain time.

Writing in *Limelight* magazine, Litson praises "the demanding vocal lines that sit above a complex, restless score, which shimmers and slides with atmospheric sounds suggesting a slithering insect-like feel, and an expressionistic style with a foreboding, ominous quality." She also notes that Director Tama Matheson "draws a highly physical performance from Simon Lobelson as Gregor, which literally sees him crawling walls and hanging from the ceiling...."

Most sadly, I can't get Down Under in time to see it.

RHINOCEROS

EXHIBIT R-1 ▸ 1973

At the five-day Jerusalem International Book Fair, the biennial Jerusalem Prize for the Freedom of the Individual in Society goes to Ionesco for *Rhinoceros*. After appearing at numerous events on the expo's crowded schedule, the playwright says of his $2,000 prize, "I earned it."

Reporting on the fair in *The New York Times,* Terence Smith describes Ionesco as "clearly accustomed to the limelight" but adds that he "squirms when asked to explain his work to others. 'Please,' he begged a student audience at the Hebrew University that seemed obsessed by his sense of despair over the human condition, 'don't take me completely seriously.'"

EXHIBIT R-2 ▸ 1974

The American Film Theatre releases its 104-minute color film of *Rhinoceros* starring Zero Mostel, Gene Wilder and Karen Black, based on a screenplay adapted by Julian Barry. Directed by Tom O'Horgan, who did *Hair* on Broadway in 1968, the movie is one of eight released by AFT as an experimental series bringing well-known dramas, such as *A Delicate Balance* and *The Iceman Cometh,* to U.S. movie theaters in brief runs. Ticket sales are largely by subscription. The venture concludes after a six-play second season.

On a personal note, my theater in Houston ends the series prematurely and I don't get to see the film version of *Rhinoceros* until finding by accident—*29 years later*—that the DVD has been released.

Purists dislike the many changes made to Ionesco's script, but there's still the magic of Mostel and Wilder, and Karen Black shines as well. The 2003 Kino Video DVD includes several added special features, such as an interview with O'Horgan and the theatrical trailer. It's still available, marked down to $12.99 last time I looked.

EXHIBIT R-3 ▸ 1990

Chichester Festival Theatre in West Sussex, England, puts on its original musical adaptation of *Rhinoceros* titled *Born Again,* starring Mandy Patinkin and José Ferrer with music by Jason Carr and libretto by Julian Barry (who did the more successful 1974 screenplay). The setting has been updated to a California shopping mall frequented by a Vietnam vet with PTSD. "Why," you may well ask. The *Chicago Tribune* rates the show "a disaster of such peculiar proportions that musical theater historians may spend years pondering how a show like 'Born Again' ever gave birth."

On the positive side, a show-goer looking back decades later posts that the production did provide a first exposure to absurdist theater.

EXHIBIT R-4 ▸ 1994

Eugene Ionesco dies at the age of 84. His obituary in *The New York Times* cites the thundering Broadway run of *Rhinoceros* in 1961 as a turning point in his career, calling it "his breakthrough play, enriched by Zero Mostel's virtuosic performance, in which he transmogrified himself from man to rhinoceros without altering his makeup or costume. Roaring, bellowing, hilarious Mostel put the playwright on the international theatrical map, and 'Rhinoceros' ran for 241 performances. But," the *Times* adds, "the play was only one of many that insured Mr. Ionesco's stature."

EXHIBIT R-5 ▸ 1996

Thirty-five years after its Broadway smash run, *Rhinoceros* has its first major New York revival at Off Broadway's Theatre Four. The adaptation by playwright Theresa Rebeck introduces some more modern props, music, and amplified rhino-worthy sound effects to achieve what Jonathan Mandell of *Newsday* calls "persuasively frightening stampedes." It's a notable first production for the non-profit start-up Valiant Theatre Company.

In his *Playbill* article about the show, David Lefkowitz notes that Ionesco was inspired both by Kafka's *Metamorphosis* and the German occupation of France, and made notes in his private journal as early as 1940 about men turning into rhinos.

EXHIBIT R-6 ▸ 2000/2010

After nearly four decades, a lengthy 1961 interview of Ionesco in French by Quebec journalist Judith Jasmin emerges on DVD, with English subtitles. Ten years later it's posted in three segments on YouTube by unidentified blogger IonescoEnthusiast.

Originally produced by Contemporary Arts Media for broadcast on Radio Canada, the video shows Ionesco discussing many topics including his childhood and education, early exposure to theater, and—especially relevant to *Rhinoceros*—his reaction to Nazism and how it differed from the reactions of so many others around him.

EXHIBIT R-7 ▸ 2001

Making its ninth season particularly memorable, Untitled Theater Company #61 produces a comprehensive Ionesco Festival at 12 New York locations with the help of about 30 other Off- and Off-Off-Broadway companies. Besides staging every one of Ionesco's 39 plays, the three-month event includes a film festival, seminars, readings and children's stories.

Edward Einhorn, Untitled's artistic director, writes that Ionesco's plays "live in a way that invites interpretation and reinterpretation. By rejecting the formal rules of theater, Ionesco has created something not completely measurable, a sort of quantum theater. It's indefinable till it's observed. Then it changes."

Films shown include the 11-minute animated short of *Rhinoceros* by Polish graphic designer Jan Lenica, produced in 1964.

EXHIBIT R-8 ▸ 2007

The year before he reads *Metamorphosis* for BBC Radio (see Exhibit M-11), Benedict Cumberbatch stars as Bérenger at London's Royal Court Theatre, the same venue at which *Rhinoceros* had its first run in the United Kingdom. *Variety* reviewer David Benedict poses the question, "Why has a play which received its U.K. premiere in 1960 directed by Orson Welles with a cast headed by Laurence Olivier languished in relative obscurity with no mainstream British revival ever since?"

He goes on to call the Royal Court production by Artistic Director Dominic Cooke "a splendid revival" that "makes the best possible case for the return of an entertaining and unsettling play."

EXHIBIT R-9 ▸ 2008

In its founding year, Baltimore's Annex Theater, which prides itself on "radical theatrical adaptations," presents its version of *Rhinoceros* in a warehouse venue. At intermission, members of the audience are directed to rotate their chairs 90 degrees to face a different stage, and some are randomly handed instruments to actively participate in Jean's transformation during the last act. The production later is posted on YouTube in 15 segments.

Romanian television news network Realitatea reports that *Rhinoceros* is the most popular play in Iran. To boost the odds of box office success at Tehran's City Theater Complex, director Farhad Aiish casts native film stars Shahab Hosseini and Ateneh Faghi-Nasiri in the lead roles. Aiish tightens the script a bit to simplify the 1950s "special prolonged style of dialogue," and he and his actress wife also join the cast.

The director acknowledges the risks that go with mounting a production focused on individualism and resistance versus totalitarianism. "The song lends itself to various interpretations," he says. "The audience will undoubtedly have its own interpretation." Realitatea's article notes that "in Iran, amid the threats of the Islamic republic's nuclear ambitions, where women who do not wear 'tchador' can not occupy the first row of the theater, the song has the resonance of a warning."

Ticket sales top 25,000 for the show's 43 performances.

Seven years after his first production of *Rhinoceros* at Théâtre de la Ville in Paris, Director Emmanuel Demarcy-Mota restages the play with the same cast but updated visual effects, architecture, and choreographed physical sequences. Live performance journal *Les Trois Coups* calls the set design "a contemporary and Kafkaesque decor ... ready to collapse" and the action a "comical ballet of bodies and words."

During the home stretch of the 2012 election season, a limited American tour (in French with English supertitles) hits four venues—Center for the Art of Performance at UCLA, Cal Performance at Berkeley, the Brooklyn Academy of Music, and the University Musical Society at the University of Michigan in Ann Arbor.

Michigan lecturer Maxime Foerster sums up the show's enduring appeal: "Unfortunately, nowadays, the rhinos depicted by Ionesco are not an endangered species, and Ionesco's fable about the tensions between resistance and conformity continues to speak to a large audience worldwide."

It's not only about 1940s France. In the *Journal of Modern Literature* (Indiana University Press), Maria Lupas lays out Ionesco's jarring experience in Bucharest while serving as a columnist for a small newspaper in the 1930s. When the editors and other intellectuals join the fascist Iron Guard, Ionesco leaves the paper, having become "increasingly isolated in his literary and political views."

Lupas says that in interviews, Ionesco "made no secret that one of his personal dramas was witnessing friends and family members succumb to the ideology of a fascist political movement in 1930s Romania." She goes on to state that *Rhinoceros* is "loosely based" on that experience, among others.

In a *New York Times* op-ed piece four years later, Valer Popa states that "the play borrows from Ionesco's own youth in Romania." He calls the Iron Guard "one of the most violent and virulently anti-Semitic organizations in that part of Europe," counting among its followers "prominent intellectuals who enthusiastically endorsed mystical jingoism and xenophobic rage."

Rhinos run on Off Off Broadway again, this time in The Seeing Place Theater's production staged at Lynn Redgrave Theater. Some of the adaptive choices made by Director Brandon Walker, who also plays Bérenger, bother reviewers. Alexa Juno says in the *OnStage* blog that the cast lacks "the verbal rhythm and physical conventions that con-vey … the absurdity of theater of the absurd" and "the heightened reality and droll nuance necessary for this particular genre." She also finds some of the added physical action distracting from Ionesco's "truly evocative writing." When the pachyderms carry protest signs as they stream through the audience from multiple angles, it muddies instead of clarifies the play's final message.

Still, Sydney Arndt writes in *Theatre Is Easy,* "Considering how politically polarized we have become, both in the U.S. and around the world, *Rhinoceros* could have been written today, and continues to speak volumes as it asks: how do we remain individuals against group mentality?" (And to think, Arndt's comment was made way back in 2016 when polarizing was just beginning to pick up speed!)

EXHIBIT R-14 ▸ 2016

Reviewing Strawberry Theatre Workshop's production less than two months before the U.S. presidential election, Rich Smith comes right out and names the elephant—er, rhinoceros—in the room. Writing in Seattle's weekly newspaper *The Stranger,* he calls the rhino a commonly used "symbol for the 20th century's worst realized -isms.... But in the context of the 2016 election, it's hard not to put a ginger wig on the pachyderm and call it Trump."

In a brilliant distillation, Smith observes that Ionesco's play portrays "logic's folly in the face of evil." He goes on to describe how "watching a character begin a scene with a desire simply to understand the rhino phenomenon and end it by growing thick skin and charging offstage disturbingly parallels the state of contemporary political discourse."

Before he's done, Smith shouts out the obvious, "the indisputable fact that we're six weeks away from Election Day and DONALD TRUMP IS THE RHINOCEROS." [Emphasis his.]

In an unusual twist for modernity's sake, the "Strawshop" casts actor-playwright Carol Louise Thompson in the normally male role of Bérenger. *Broadway World* calls the move "brilliant," saying "she felt like a skittish rabbit amongst a herd of rhinos, and it really worked."

EXHIBIT R-15 ▸ 2016–PRESENT

Alas! Here's a behavior-based connection that is painfully logical. A Google Images search on the words "rhino" and "Trump" or "GOP" simultaneously is guaranteed to net some nasty political cartoons and Photoshopped images showing Potus 45's head or face on a rhino's body, or a rhinoceros partying on the White House lawn—or even a Trump-noceros defecating wherever it likes. (Coincidentally, the soundalike acronym "RINO" gets co-opted for "Republicans in Name Only.")

Political cartoonists, graphic artists and web iconographers, both amateur and professional, go to town with endless variations, replacing the obsolescent elephant with the ready-to-rumble rhinoceros in the star-festooned red-white-and-blue logo of the Retrumplican Party. It's a sad but understandable graphic transition.

What would the prophet Ionesco have to say to us now?

EXHIBIT R~16 ▸ 2017

Nozhorns are on the rampage in the first Yiddish staging of *Rhinoceros*, presented Off Broadway by the New Yiddish Rep at the Castillo Theatre. Director Moshe Yassur's production with English supertitles uses a new Yiddish translation by Eli Rosen, who also plays Jean. The Rep bills itself as a "laboratory on the front line of resistance against the extinction of Eastern European Yiddish theater." Its website addresses the timeliness of Ionesco's play: "The other day Trump used the phrase 'my followers.' That says it all. Every theater in the country that cares about freedom, human rights, and our way of life ought to produce this play. Hitler came to power in 1933 with only 36% of the vote. By 1939 he brought on a World War. Lets [sic] hope we don't start seeing rhinoceroses in the streets. The folks in Charlottesville already have."

The large doctored photo below that commentary shows the facade of The White House draped with red Nazi-style banners featuring a rhino silhouette, a rhino flag flapping in the breeze atop the building, and its current occupant on the lawn wearing a red rhino-logoed armband.

New York Times critic Alexis Soloski finds some rough edges in the production, yet says it's worth attending. In her review, she advises resistors to call their elected officials, march in protests, vote—and "above all, try not to turn into an odd-toed ungulate."

EXHIBIT R~17 ▸ 2017

Picking up the political theme and stampeding with it, Houston's Catastrophic Theatre does a one-month run of *Rhinoceros,* which Director Tamarie Cooper first experienced as a student at the city's High School for the Performing and Visual Arts. She says "after last year's election, we all felt like, well, we need to do *Rhinoceros* now…." Catastrophic's minute-and-a-quarter promotional video is a quick parade of raging rhinos, goose-stepping storm troopers, crowds and mobs of many kinds, interspersed with star Kyle Sturdivant's virtuosic facial contortions as he tries to fight off his inevitable metamorphosis.

The Houston Chronicle calls Sturdivant's portrayal of rhinocerization "terrifying and intoxicating." Writing for *The Houston Press,* Jessica Goldman points out that Catastrophic (under an earlier name) had done the play 14 years earlier. "While there's nothing disturbing about remounting a work, it is upsetting that this particular play needed to be dusted off and brought back." She also gives fine analysis of the mental process bringing calm to the witnessing populace:

> It's all very amusing, this intellectual normalcy of the sudden presence of rhinos in their midst. Until it isn't. More upsetting than the population's transformation into rhinos is the reaction of the holdout humans. Name an excuse for not sounding the alarm or nipping the situation in the bud and Ionesco throws it at us. The rhinos aren't real (fake news), it's a temporary thing, they'll come around (denial), stop worrying and learn to be more detached (head in sand), well there is nothing we can do anyway (resignation), hey, don't the rhinos look happy? They don't seem insane (acceptance).

EXHIBIT R‑18 ▸ 2018

Through the magic of audible and visible special effects, and plenty of spoken suggestion, productions of *Rhinoceros* manage to get audiences to experience close encounters with not one, or a pair, but rushing hordes of the armored beasts. However, in their dwindling natural habitats in the wild, real rhinos are fading fast. They may soon join the unicorn as a wondrous but non-existent group of species.

Becoming the dodo of ungulates, this frightening tank of a mammal is relentlessly being wiped out faster than conservationists can come up with solutions. As a conservationist myself, as well as a fan of Ionesco, I find this wholly unacceptable. It would be immoral to be a devotee of Ionesco's metaphorical *Rhinoceros* and at the same time ignore what is happening to real rhinos in their native lands.

If you share my anguish, please read my Coda for Conservation devoted to this issue. It has nothing directly to do with literary criticism, but it's so important I've tacked it on as a supplement following the summary of my thesis findings. In addition, I will donate any and all proceeds from the sale of this publication (after bookseller commissions) to support rhino conservation and protection.

EXHIBIT R-19 ▸ 2019

British publisher Alma Books announces release through its Calder imprint of a collection titled *The Bérenger Plays,* bringing together in a single volume the four works featuring Ionesco's "everyman protagonist Jean Bérenger"—*The Killer, Exit the King, Strolling in the Air,* and *Rhinoceros.* All four were completed in about a five-year period in the late 1950s to early 60s.

While each play is unique and the same-in-name characters have no continuity, each drama shows "themes that preoccupied Ionesco throughout his career, such as mortality, alienation, freedom and the evils of Fascism." Translations are by Donald Watson and Derek Prouse.

SUMMARY—WHAT I LEARNED

It would be a work's worst fate to be forgotten—to sit on library shelves without being checked out; to be returned to the publishing house as unsold inventory; to go decade after decade unstaged; and to fade from the awareness of the reading and playgoing public other than the most diehard scholars. I didn't expect either *Metamorphosis* or *Rhinoceros* to fall that far; in fact, I hoped they were remaining reasonably popular as classics of their respective genres. This semi-centennial thesis revival exercise was meant to satisfy my concern about how the two were doing.

Apparently, I needn't have worried. Both works are leading exceedingly rich lives! In 1967, when everything was still pretty simple and straightforward, they existed as hardbound and paperback books, and an occasional stage production. That was mostly it. As my quick survey of events in the ongoing career of each reveals (per exhibits M-1 through M-22 and R-1 through R-19), the accelerating cultural explosion since then has only enriched the literary and theatrical environment, encouraging all manner of adaptation, experimenting, multimedia-izing, cross-media development, and translation, and that doesn't even bring up the advent of the Internet with its instant availability of virtually anything anywhere.

This is not to say that everything covered by that long list is necessarily well done or an improvement on the original works, but the existence of all the new versions of Kafka's and Ionesco's works shows how much they continue to capture the modern imagination, inspiring new readers and viewers, translators and directors, actors and dancers, authors and filmmakers, composers and choreographers, designers and cartoonists, reviewers and bloggers, students and teachers—even grizzled former thesis-writers. And of course, the unfortunate political climate of the 2000s' second decade has stimulated an intense new level of interest in *Rhinoceros*. A quick Internet search reveals live theater productions are building significant mass all over the United States and in many other countries. It's definitely becoming a stampede!

Yes, my conclusion is simple. This pair of my favorite works is thriving just fine, and in many ways that we could not have imagined 50 years ago. I expect whoever follows up in 2067 will have even more to report than I do here. I just hope someone figures out how to forward the findings to me when the time comes.

CODA FOR CONSERVATION

It is sadly ironic that rhinoceros the animal is going extinct at the same time that rhinoceros the political animal, loudly portrayed in Ionesco's play, is running more and more rampant.

The idea that the horn of a rhinoceros, no matter from which species, has curative powers dates back many, many centuries, at least for some ailments. For other conditions, rhino horn may have been added to the list of "traditional" medicines in the last 200 years or less. Contrary to widespread belief, its use as an aphrodisiac is *not* part of traditional Oriental medicine but may have popped up in recent years as a Viagra alternative in Asia *because of* mentions in misinformed Western media.

In any case, in spite of spotty attempts by some governments to shut down the legal trade in rhino horn or to stockpile humanely harvested horn, poaching remains the most serious threat to the rhino's survival. Adding to the pressure (but on a smaller scale) is non-medicinal demand for horn, such as making carved ornamental objects in China and handles of traditional, curved jambiya daggers in Yemen.

Tragically, the decline in the world's remaining rhino populations only serves to worsen the surge in black-market prices for horn, encouraging more risk-taking by poachers. It's a heartless cycle, full of hopes and setbacks. In the not-too-distant future there may be viewers of Ionesco's drama who grew up on an Earth totally devoid of rhinos. They'll be as extinct as the centrosauruses, somewhat rhino-like one-horned, herbivorous dinosaurs that died out 70 million years ago. It won't be due to a meteor striking our planet; it will come from one more colossal and irreversible human failure.

More than ever in our history, animals need love, respect, rights, advocacy and protection. At this point, I'm all for animal suffrage and citizenship, but that will be a whole 'nother project.

Meanwhile, I hope you read my conservation exhibits that follow.

EXHIBIT C-1 ▶ 500 BCE–2018

Traditional Chinese medicine dates back more than two millennia, and sometime early in that history, unfortunately, rhinoceros horn enters its pharmacopoeia. Even though the substance of the horn— keratin—is identical to human fingernail, it is still considered by many in several Asian countries to be a cure for any of a long list of ailments: gout, boils, fever, rheumatism, typhoid, liver ailments, headache, snakebite, food poisoning, hallucination, hangover, and recently, even cancer. To dispense as medication, powder or shavings from ground-up horn are dissolved in water. Scientific tests fail repeatedly to detect any health efficacy in the supposed remedy, and in 1993 China's Ministry of Health removes rhino horn from its list of acceptable medicines.

Yet, here we are, nearly in the third decade of the Twenty-first Century, and the demand not only persists but expands, particularly in Vietnam where both wealth and alcohol consumption are growing rapidly. Since about 2005, a rumor circulates that an unnamed former politician in Vietnam is cured of an unspecified cancer by taking rhino horn. It creates a clamor for horn-based cancer treatment, which is understandable since the country has hardly any radiotherapy units to serve its population. On top of that, the aphrodisiac myth pushed by Western media helps turn rhino horn into a recreational drug in Vietnam, where it's also claimed to allow heavier drinking sans hangover, and becomes a handy currency for paying bribes.

For all these reasons, the value of rhino horn there and in many other Asian countries reaches parity ounce-for-ounce with gold, and the drive to poach in Asia and Africa charges on. Can't afford to pay that kind of price? Try chewing your nails for a quick keratin fix. The alleged cure-all's been right at your fingertips all along!

The world, says Nicky Reeves in *The Guardian,* is "full of beliefs and practices which are irrational, superstitious, or without scientific validity, but that does not mean that they are necessarily traditional.... It is often the case that promoters of a medicine or foodstuff might have an interest in giving it a historical or traditional pedigree, but such claims need to be critically assessed rather than uncritically reproduced." The article continues with a hopeful tone.

> Devastating as it is to the welfare and survival of rhino species, the Vietnamese market for rhino horns is both faddish and reversible. Education and marketing campaigns that try to make its consumption socially unacceptable are as achievable in Vietnam as campaigns were [in] the UK to make once popular practices like as drink-driving [Brit-speak for "drunk driving" or "DWI"] socially unacceptable. This has been done for rhino horns before: in the 1970s and 1980s,

the Yemeni demand for rhino horn dagger handles also had a devastating effect on rhino populations.... A mixture of legal measures and social pressure, sometimes from the highest levels of the Yemeni state, coupled with awareness campaigns about harm done to rhinos in the wild, were fairly effective in making the practice of gifting daggers with rhino horn handles socially unacceptable. Whether rhino horn dagger handles were 'traditional' or not, it was clearly possible to confront the practice.

Back in 2010, meanwhile, the last surviving Javan rhino in Vietnam is killed. Maybe the awareness campaigns can still help the remaining species in Africa.

EXHIBIT C-2 ▶ 2009

Drawing on his experience in corporate communications and cause-related marketing, as well as his keen interest in conservation of endangered species worldwide, the author sends a proposal to one of the planet's largest pharmaceutical companies hoping to spark interest in sponsoring a campaign to reduce the rate of rhinoceros poaching. The concept: to lower the demand for rhino horn in countries where significant numbers believe it has aphrodisiac powers by providing medical facts on male performance while also promoting the company's market-leading erectile dysfunction drug as a more effective and environmentally benign solution. Payback would be positive vibes usable in corporate and product advertising around the world, following the model of Exxon's "Save the Tiger" campaign begun in the 1990s.

For whatever reason (perhaps the correspondence never made it past the mail room), the pharmaceutical company fails to respond, and due to lack of time the author lets the matter drop. Although the rational appeal of my marketing idea persists, my recent research has taught me that most demand for rhino horn over the past 2,000 years has had nothing to do with sexual issues. Oh well....

EXHIBIT C-3 ▸ 2013

At a cost of $15,000, the World Wildlife Fund donates microchips to embed in the horns of the more than 1,000 rhinoceroses living in Kenya, plus five scanners that will enable wildlife officials to trace the origin of any poached horns that are recovered. Tracking and tranquilizing the beasts to fit them with the chips brings additional costs. The project reflects the escalating war between poachers and conservationists.

The Kenya Wildlife Service says in a statement, "Investigators will be able to link any poaching case to a recovered or confiscated horn, and this forms crucial evidence in court, contributing towards the prosecution's ability to push for sentencing of a suspected rhino criminal."

The rapid rise in poaching even spills over into the heavily guarded Nairobi National Park, where a white rhino is shot dead for the first time in six years. In South Africa's Kruger National Park, authorities turn to drones while poachers gain advantage through night-vision goggles and helicopters.

EXHIBIT C-4 ▸ 2015

Technology in its many forms plays an increasing role in the war against rhino poaching, as black market prices for horn hit $30,000 *per pound*. (A single horn can weigh three to four pounds. Do the math!) One new approach is to manufacture lab-grown, genetically engineered synthetic horn that can pass for the real thing, the idea being to flood the market and deflate prices. Another is to inject horns on living rhinos with dye and chemicals that don't harm the animals but make the horn unmarketable as decoration because of discoloration and as medicine because of severe side effects.

In South Africa's national parks, a British not-for-profit called Protect begins implanting rhino heart monitors and miniature flush-mounted, in-horn video cameras. Whenever a radio collar detects an elevated heart rate, it sends an alert with GPS data so anti-poaching rangers can immediately drive or fly to the rhino's location and head off any evildoers.

EXHIBIT C~5 ▸ 2017

John Hume, a rancher in South Africa, aims to breed 200 rhinos annually on his 20,000-acre Buffalo Dream Ranch in order to save the species by removing horns every other year and selling the harvest legally, which he claims will eliminate the incentive to poach. Hume's rhino herd numbers about 1,500 and his cache of removed horns already amounts to some six tons, worth millions. Leading rhino conservationists and organizations vehemently disagree with his anti-poaching theory, asserting that legally purchased horn is likely to be exported illegally and feed the cycle of demand. Nonetheless, Hume successfully lobbies his government, which finally lifts its moratorium on the horn trade within South Africa.

Writing in *The Telegraph,* Nigel Richardson says about rhino horn, "It may be prized in the East for its medicinal properties but it has none, which means the global criminal operation that threatens to slaughter a species is based on a myth. By doing what he is doing, Hume is 'perpetuating' that myth...."

EXHIBIT C~6 ▸ 2018

With only two female northern white rhinos left in the world and the last surviving male recently deceased, the Leibnitz Institute for Zoo and Wildlife Research in Berlin announces it has created two test tube embryos using southern white rhino eggs and stored northern sperm. The resulting hybrid is a test run to prove the in vitro method works. Next, subject to approval by Kenya, comes extraction of fresh eggs from those last two northern females to produce pure northern embryos to implant in southern surrogate moms. The total southern white rhino population is about 21,000.

Plenty of challenges remain for the project, not the least of which is creating genetic diversity among the lab-generated offspring via stem cell techniques, which could take 10 years or more, assuming the creatures grow to maturity in zoos. Long seen as a last hope for saving species from extinction, in vitro so far has worked only for giant pandas, Asian elephants and the black-footed ferret.

EXHIBIT C-7 ▸ 2018

China reverses course by legalizing the use of tiger and rhino parts in certain hospitals, supposedly sourced from farmed animals. Conservationists argue that it's hard to be sure parts don't come from victims of poaching. Humane Society International says China "has signed a death warrant for imperiled rhinos and tigers in the wild who already face myriad threats to their survival," calling the move "essentially a laundering scheme for illegal tiger bone and rhino horn to enter the marketplace and further perpetuate the demand for these animal parts."

The World Federation of Chinese Medicine Societies removes tiger bone and rhino horn from its list of approved treatments, but will buyers even notice—or care?

EXHIBIT C-8 ▸ 2018

In a tragic translocation disaster, eight of 11 black rhinos being moved from two of Kenya's national parks to a third park to help preserve the species die of saltwater poisoning. In the previous 13 years, Kenya had relocated 149 rhinos and lost only eight, so this incident is considered a major loss. More than one-tenth of the world's 5,000 remaining black rhinos reside in Kenya.

Mourning the tragedy, Paula Kahumbu, CEO of WildLifeDirect, says "Moving rhinos is complicated, akin to moving gold bullion; it requires extremely careful planning and security due to the value of these rare animals."

EXHIBIT C-9 ▸ 2018

In an unusually karmic twist, Nature fights back with punishment befitting the crime as a group of lions at the Sibuya Game Preserve in South Africa turns three would-be rhino poachers into dinner. The next morning, police and the anti-poaching patrol are unsure how many victims there are, but they do find six boots and six gloves, along with a backpack full of food, a high-powered rifle with silencer, an axe and a wire cutter. Investigators surmise the suspected poachers may have stumbled upon the pride of lions after dark and tried to run. To run from a lion is a surefire way to say "I am prey—eat me!"

In South Africa, conviction for rhino poaching means jail time, yet in 2017 more than 1,000 of the animals were taken illegally. Although that's a slight decline compared to 2016, it's still a loss of nearly three rhinos every single day. In the decade ended in 2017, more than 7,100 were killed in South Africa alone. Drought in the southern part of the African continent may worsen the rhino's population decline in 2018.

EXHIBIT C-10 ▸ 2018

Once nearly wiped out, the great one-horned rhino (*rhinoceros unicornis*) now is populous enough in India and Nepal to have frequent run-ins with rice farmers and other humans when outside their preserves. An Indian company called Elrhino, founded seven years ago, provides residents of eight villages near the Pobitora Wildlife Sanctuary a financial interest in rhino preservation. The locals gather rhino dung, which the beasts deposit in great mounds, to use in the manufacture of luxury paper goods. The company even buys the dung from farmers whose crops have been damaged by foraging rhinos or their hooves to lessen animosity toward the animals.

Both rhinos and elephants leave a lot of undigested grass fiber in their droppings. Once thoroughly cleaned, that fiber is mixed with various other materials. Elrhino is not yet turning a profit but has found a market for its products in the U.S., Hong Kong, Great Britain and Switzerland.

EXHIBIT C-11 ▸ 2018

Dateline for good news on the captive breeding front: The Watani Grasslands Reserve of the North Carolina Zoo in Asheboro, where not one, but two baby southern white rhinos are delivered 11 days apart. Christened Bonnie and Nandi, both female calves reside in the 40-acre, Africa-like tall tree savannah created during a major renovation 13 years earlier at a cost of $8.7 million. The calves share their space with five other rhinos, a herd of elephants, and numerous ostrich and antelope.

The rhinos have plenty of real turf, mud wallows, and even a spinning punching bag for butting practice. One of the goals of the reserve's expansion was to enhance breeding success for both rhinos and elephants, which face a similar onslaught of poachers in the wild.

EXHIBIT C-12 ▸ 2018

Want to help the cause of rhino conservation? There are many organizations, large and small, worthy of your support. Here are just a few of the ones I've come across.

Save the Rhino International
Based in London, SRI operates projects in several countries of Africa and Asia to protect all rhino species and, where possible, increase their populations. The organization equips anti-poaching rangers; supports canine squads to track and capture poachers, detect illegal wildlife products and recover stolen property; funds veterinary services and electronic wildlife tracking; and works to reduce demand for illegal rhino horn. [savetherhino.org]

International Rhino Foundation
The IRF protects particularly threatened rhino populations in the wild and supports applied research that aims to improve the chances for long-term survival of all rhino species. Founded in 1989, the foundation's program office is in Strasburg, Virginia and its business office is in Fort Worth, Texas. [rhinos.org]

International Anti-Poaching Foundation
This group employs modern tactics and technologies to defend wildlife from the crisis-level threat of poaching within protected areas. Since anti-poaching actions alone won't solve the crisis facing endangered species including rhinos, the IAPF also works with partners specializing in community engagement, research and development, wildlife rescue and biodiversity management. Founded in 2009, the IAPF is registered in Australia, South Africa, Zimbabwe, and the United States with an office in Arlington, Virginia. [iapf.org]

Helping Rhinos
Registered as a charity in the U.K. and a 501(c)(3) in the U.S. (Helping Rhinos USA), Helping Rhinos supports anti-poaching teams, education and awareness programs, sanctuaries and rhino orphanages. Donation opportunities include a number of options to adopt a rhino or a patrol dog and to support an anti-poaching team. The group extended its work in 2015 by launching the Rhino Alliance. [helpingrhinos.org]

Rhino Alliance
This international coalition of about a dozen not-for-profit organizations committed to protecting rhinos joined forces to share resources and best practices, understand each other's work and avoid duplication of effort. So far the alliance has member organizations from South Africa, Vietnam, the United States, the United Kingdom and the Isle of Man. Its activities are overseen by Helping Rhinos and donations must be made to the individual entities. [rhinoalliance.org]

Rhino Ark
This Kenyan charitable trust has worked in conjunction with the Kenya Wildlife Service to develop electric fences around very large areas of land to prevent loss of wildlife, principally rhinos and elephants, due to negative interaction with humans. Its largest fence project cost $10 million and took a decade to build. The trust is also active fostering community involvement in conservation and monitors a number of Kenyan environmental and sustainability issues. [rhinoark.org]

For Rangers
The rangers who work to protect endangered wildlife in Africa put their lives on the line every day, and more than 100 of them are killed each year by poachers. To look after these brave individuals patrolling for 10 or more conservation organizations, For Rangers raises funds primarily through ultra-marathons and other extreme athletic endurance events. Proceeds have bought boots and uniforms, life insurance, fitness equipment, binoculars, camouflage, thermal imaging systems, solar power, medical kits and even a kitchen and lounge. [forrangers.com]

WEBLIOGRAPHY

All of my research for this 50-year thesis update was Internet-based. The sources I used appear below, arranged by exhibit number and in a form of my own creating that may not conform to the most widely accepted style guides. (I'm retired and a volunteer scholar, so I can do that.) References include headline or title, source publication or organization, byline (if any), and date of publication (if provided), followed by the URL and date I visited.

EXHIBIT M-1 ▶ 1969/1989

"Steven Berkoff premieres" / iainfisher.com. [iainfisher.com/berkoff/berkoff-premieres.html] 10/7/18.

"Review/Theater; Baryshnikov in 'Metamorphosis'" / *The New York Times*. By Frank Rich, March 7, 1989. [nytimes.com/1989/03/07/theater/review-theater-baryshnikov-in-metamorphosis.html] 10/8/18.

EXHIBIT M-2 ▶ 1975

"Die Verwandlung (1975)" / IMDb. [imdb.com/title/tt0174019/?ref_=ttfc_fc_tt] 10/19/18.

"Jan Nemec Biography" / IMDb. [imdb.com/name/nm0625866/bio?ref_=nm_ov_bio_sm] 11/14/18.

"Franz Kafka—Dönüsüm / die Verwandlung (Türkçe Alt Yazili)" / YouTube. [youtube.com/watch?v=eHVf2LSBHtU] 11/14/18.

"Czech New Wave Films and Movie Memorabilia" / Classic Art Films. [classicartfilms.com/film-movements/czech-new-wave] 11/15/18.

EXHIBIT M-3 ▶ 1976

"Metamorphosis (1976)" / IMDb. [imdb.com/title/tt0074561/?ref_=tt_rec_tt] 10/19/18.

"Ivo Dvorák" / IMDb. [imdb.com/name/nm0245371/?ref_=tt_ov_wr] 11/15/18.

"Ivo Dvorák" / The Swedish Film Database: / Swedish Film Institute. [svenskfilmdatabas.se/en/item/?type=person&itemid=70817#films] 11/15/18.

"Forvandlingen (1975)" / AllMovie. [allmovie.com/movie/forvandlingen-v156066] 11/15/18.

EXHIBIT M-4 ▸ 1978

"The Metamorphosis of Mr. Samsa (1978)" / IMDb. [imdb.com/title/tt0076389/?ref_=tt_rec_tt] 10/19/18.

EXHIBIT M-5 ▸ 1983

Howard, Brian, "Metamorphosis (1983)" / Boosey & Hawkes. [boosey.com/pages/opera/moreDetails?musicID=5211] 10/4/18.

Feature, "Brian Howard traces the history of Metamorphosis" / Opera Australia. [opera.org.au/home/productions/metamorphosis/brian-howard-history] 10/4/18.

EXHIBIT M-6 ▸ 1988

"Solo Piano (Philip Glass album)" / Wikipedia. [en.wikipedia.org/wiki/Solo_Piano_(Philip_Glass_album)] 10/20/18.

"Philip Glass: I'm drawn to Kafka's darkness" / *The Telegraph*. [telegraph.co.uk/culture/music/opera/7998330/Philip-Glass-Im-drawn-to-Kafkas-darkness.html] 10/20/18.

Philip Glass, "Metamorphosis, for piano" / AllMusic. Description by Jeremy Grimshaw. [allmusic.com/composition/metamorphosis-for-piano-mc0002361548] 10/20/18.

EXHIBIT M-7 ▸ 2000

Metamorph Simpsons / Wikisimpsons. [simpsonswiki.com/wiki/Metamorph_Simpsons] 10/20/18.

The Simpsons' Treehouse of Horror / Wikisimpsons. [simpsonswiki.com/wiki/The_Simpsons%27_Treehouse_of_Horror] 10/20/18.

"Café Kafka" / Simpsons Wiki. [simpsons.wikia.com/wiki/Caf%C3%A9_Kafka] 10/20/18.

"Where Did THAT Come From—Cafe Kafka" / *The Simpsons Tapped Out Addicts*. Posted by The Wookiie, May 18, 2017. [tstoaddicts.com/2017/05/18/where-did-that-come-from-cafe-kafka/] 10/20/18.

EXHIBIT M-8 ▸ 2002

"The world was his Roach Motel; a raid on Kafka's Metamorphosis"/ *The Christian Science Monitor*. By Ron Charles, February 14, 2002. [csmonitor.com/2002/0214/p15s01-bogn.html] 10/21/18.

"The Top 100 Books of the Year" / *SFGate*. December 15, 2002. [sfgate.com/books/article/THE-TOP-100-BOOKS-OF-THE-YEAR-2745667.php] 10/21/18.

"Marc Estrin" / Wikipedia. [en.wikipedia.org/wiki/Marc_Estrin] 10/20/18.

EXHIBIT M-9 ▸ 2003

"The Metamorphosis By Franz Kafka, adapted by Peter Kuper." [penguinrandomhouse.com/books/96229/the-metamorphosis-by-franz-kafka-adapted-by-peter-kuper/9781400052998/] 10/21/18.

EXHIBIT M-10 ▸ 2006

Fiction, "A Bug's Life" / *The Washington Post*. By Ron Charles, January 7, 2007. [washingtonpost.com/wp-dyn/content/article/2007/01/05/AR2007010500083.html?noredirect=on] 10/9/18.

"Kockroach" / Wikipedia. [en.wikipedia.org/wiki/Kockroach] 10/22/18.

"Metamorphosis, Franz Kafka" / Audio CD. [penguin.co.uk/books/1115514/metamorphosis/9781785299933.html] 10/22/18.

"Metamorphosis: A BBC Radio 4 Reading" / Audible Audiobook – Abridged. [amazon.com/Metamorphosis-BBC-Radio-4-Reading/dp/B0754HG7Q4/ref=sr_1_1?ie=UTF8&qid=1540522609&sr=1-1&keywords=Kafka+Cumberbatch&dpID=51bZtBogFuL&preST=_SX342_QL70_&dpSrc=srch] 10/25/18.

"List of Benedict Cumberbatch performances" / Wikipedia. [en.wikipedia.org/wiki/List_of_Benedict_Cumberbatch_performances] 10/22/18.

EXHIBIT M-12 ▸ 2010

"Metamorphosis Immersive Kafka—Full Movie" / YouTube. [youtube.com/watch?v=fHKk4GRquOY] 10/7/18.

"Metamorphosis: Immersive Kafka (2010)" / IMDb. [imdb.com/title/tt1667844/?ref_=ttspec_spec_tt] 10/7/18.

"Metamorphosis: Towards Immersive Interactive Film" / ResearchGate. By Barnabás Takács, 2018. [researchgate.net/publication/268255096_METAMORPHOSIS_Towards_Immersive_Interactive_Film] 10/23/18.

"Metamorphosis—A 360° Immersive Film Wins Hollywood Award" / CISION PRWeb. December 10, 2010. [prweb.com/releases/2010/12/prweb4877714.htm] 10/23/18.

EXHIBIT M-13 ▸ 2011/2013

"Arthur Pita, Choreographer" / Royal Opera House. [roh.org.uk/people/arthur-pita] 10/27/18.

"The Metamorphosis" / arthurpita.com. [arthurpita.com/works/the-metamorphosis/] 10/25/18.

"Arthur Pita and Edward Watson: On Metamorphosis" / *The Ballet Bag*. [theballetbag.com/2011/09/16/arthur-pita-edward-watson-on-metamorphosis/] 10/27/18.

Dance, "The Metamorphosis—review" / *The Guardian*. By Judith Mackrel, September 22, 2011. [theguardian.com/stage/2011/sep/22/the-metamorphosis-dance-review] 10/27/18.

"A Tale's Kafkaesque Transformation" / *The New York Times*. By Roslyn Sulcas, August 30, 2013. [nytimes.com/2013/09/01/arts/dance/edward-watson-and-arthur-pita-create-the-metamorphosis.html] 10/27/18.

EXHIBIT M-14 ▸ 2012/2016

"Metamorphosis (2012)" / IMDb. [imdb.com/title/tt2319941/fullcredits/?ref_=tt_ov_st_sm] 10/19/18.

"Metamorphosis (2012 Film)" / Wikipedia. [en.wikipedia.org/wiki/Metamorphosis_(2012_film)] 10/19/18.

"Metamorphosis—Centenary Edition—The Film" / Attractive Features. [metamorphosisonfilm.com/#hello] 10/25/18.

"Metamorphosis: Film Review" / *The Hollywood Reporter*. By John DeFore, August 31, 2012. [hollywoodreporter.com/review/metamorphosis-montreal-review-367290] 10/25/18.

"Metamorphosis undergoes a metamorphosis" / *Undead Backbrain*. By Robert Hood, December 10, 2016. [roberthood.net/blog/index.php/2016/12/10/metamorphosis-undergoes-a-metamorphosis/] 10/26/18.

"Metamorphosis: Unleashing the bug—Exclusive" / *Undead Backbrain*. By Robert Hood, January 1, 2011. [roberthood.net/blog/index.php/2011/01/01/metamorphosis-unleashing-the-bug-exclusive/] 10/26/18.

"Franz Kafka: Google Doodle honors famed novelist's birthday" / IMDb. By editorial@zap2it.com, July 3, 2013. [imdb.com/news/ni55879664?ref_=tt_nwr1] 10/12/18.

"Franz Kafka's 130th birthday marked by a Google-homepage metamorphosis" / *National Post.* By *National Post* staff, July 3, 2013. [nationalpost.com/news/franz-kafkas-130th-birthday-marked-by-a-google-homepage-metamorphosis] 10/12/18.

"Google Search Statistics" / internet live stats. [internetlivestats.com/google-search-statistics/#trend] 10/12/18.

"How many Google searches per day on average in 2018?" / Ardor Seo. [ardorseo.com/blog/how-many-google-searches-per-day-2018/] 10/12/18.

"Samsa in Love" / *The New Yorker.* By Haruki Murakami (translated from the Japanese by Ted Goossen), October 28, 2013. [newyorker.com/magazine/2013/10/28/samsa-in-love] 1/17/19.

"New From Murakami: Tales of Cool Cars, Shinto Spirits and Lost Love" / *The New York Times.* By Jay Fielden, May 9, 2017. [nytimes.com/2017/05/09/books/review/men-without-women-haruki-murakami.html] 1/17/19.

"Haruki Murakami" / Wikipedia. [en.wikipedia.org/wiki/Haruki_Murakami] 1/17/19.

"Review: 'Men Without Women' by Haruki Murakami" / *Chicago Tribune.* By Shoshana Olidort, May 8, 2017. [chicagotribune.com/lifestyles/books/sc-men-without-women-haruki-murakami-books-0510-20170508-story.html] 1/17/19.

EXHIBIT M-17 ▸ 2014

"On Translating Kafka's 'The Metamorphosis'" / *The New Yorker.* By Susan Bernofsky, January 14, 2014. [newyorker.com/books/page-turner/on-translating-kafkas-the-metamorphosis] 10/2/18.

"The Metamorphosis, A New Translation by Susan Bernofsky" / W.W. Norton & Company, Inc. [books.wwnorton.com/books/detail.aspx?ID=4294977469] 10/2/18.

Books blog, Franz Kafka, "Kafka's Metamorphosis and its mutations in translation" / *The Guardian.* By WB Gooderham, May 13, 2015. [theguardian.com/books/booksblog/2015/may/13/kafka-metamorphosis-translations] 1/29/19.

EXHIBIT M-18 ▸ 2014/2017

"Why David Lynch Backed Away From Transforming Kafka's The Metamorphosis Into a Movie" / *Syfy Wire.* Contributed by Benjamin Bullard, November 7, 2017. [syfy.com/syfywire/why-david-lynch-backed-away-from-transforming-kafka%E2%80%99s-the-metamorphosis-into-a-movie] 10/30/18.

"David Lynch Explains Why He's Given Up On Adapting 'Metamorphosis'"/ *The Playlist.* By Kevin Jagernauth, November 6, 2017. [theplaylist.net/david-lynch-metamorphosis-20171106/] 10/3/18.

EXHIBIT M-19 ▸ 2015

"In the Shadow Of Kafka: David Baddiel explores The Metamorphosis for new BBC radio series" / *The Independent.* By Boyd Tonkin, May 7, 2015. [independent.co.uk/arts-entertainment/tv/features/in-the-shadow-of-kafka-david-baddiel-explores-the-metamorphosis-for-new-bbc-radio-series-10233524.html] 10/2/18.

EXHIBIT M-20 ▸ 2015

"Die Verwandlung (2015)" / de.wikipedia.org. [de.wikipedia.org/wiki/Die_Verwandlung_(2015)] 10/30/18.

"Die Verwandlung (2015)" / IMDb. [imdb.com/title/tt4195258/?ref_=tt_rec_tt] 10/2/18.

Kurzfilm, "Die Verwandlung" / BR Fernsehen (Bavarian Radio Television). [br.de/br-fernsehen/sendungen/kurzfilm/verwandlung-igor-plischke-kurzfilm100.html] 10/30/18.

"Die Verwandlung, A Film by Igor Plischke" / aug&ohr medien (film festival agency). [augohr.de/catalogue/die-verwandlung] 10/30/18.

EXHIBIT M-21 ▶ 2016
"Based on The Metamorphosis, A Short Story by Franz Kafka, Metamorphosis, A Game from Mito Studio." [metamorphos.is/] 2/1/19.

EXHIBIT M-22 ▶ 2018
Feature, "Brian Howard traces the history of Metamorphosis" / Opera Australia. [opera.org.au/home/productions/metamorphosis/brian-howard-history] 10/4/18.

Reviews, "Metamorphosis (Opera Australia)" / *Limelight.* By Jo Litson, September 27, 2018. [limelightmagazine.com.au/reviews/metamorphosis-opera-australia/] 10/4/18.

EXHIBIT R-1 ▶ 1973
"Jerusalem Prize" / Wikipedia. [en.wikipedia.org/wiki/Jerusalem_Prize] 1/19/19.

"Jerusalem: Prize for a Friend, Ionesco" / *The New York Times.* By Terence Smith, May 14, 1973. [nytimes.com/1973/05/14/archives/jerusalem-prize-for-a-friend-ionesco.html] 1/18/19.

EXHIBIT R-2 ▶ 1974
"Rhinoceros (1974)" / IMDb. [imdb.com/title/tt0070605/] 11/5/18.

"American Film Theatre" / Wikipedia. [en.wikipedia.org/wiki/American_Film_Theatre] 11/5/18.

"Tom O'Horgan" / Wikipedia. [en.wikipedia.org/wiki/Tom_O%27Horgan] 11/5/18.

"Rhinoceros Directed by Tom O'Horgan" / Kino Lorber. [kinolorber.com/film/rhinoceros] 11/17/18.

EXHIBIT R-3 ▸ 1990

"Pity the Rhinos" / *Chicago Tribune*. By Matt Wolf, September 23, 1990. [chicagotribune.com/news/ct-xpm-1990-09-23-9003190604-story.html] 11/5/18.

"History: The 1990s" / Pass It On / Chichester Festival Theatre. By Holly Stewart. [passiton.cft.org.uk/about-cft/the-1990s/] 11/6/18.

"Your Memories (Continued)" / Pass It On / Chichester Festival Theatre. By Anon, June 15, 2015. [passiton.cft.org.uk/make-a-nomination/page/14/] 11/6/18.

EXHIBIT R-4 ▸ 1994

Archives 1994, "Eugene Ionesco Is Dead at 84; Stage's Master of Surrealism" / *The New York Times*. By Mel Gussow, March 29, 1994. [nytimes.com/1994/03/29/obituaries/eugene-ionesco-is-dead-at-84-stage-s-master-of-surrealism.html] 11/2/18.

EXHIBIT R-5 ▸ 1996

"Theresa Rebeck Revamps *Rhinoceros* for Valiant" / *Playbill*. By David Lefkowitz, October 11, 1996. [playbill.com/article/theresa-rebeck-revamps-rhinoceros-for-valiant-com-68542] 11/2/18.

EXHIBIT R-6 ▸ 2000/2010

"Interview with Ionesco part 1" / YouTube. Posted by IonescoEnthusiast, April 24, 2010. [youtube.com/watch?v=Qih8bwcfh1U] 10/1/18.

"Interview with Ionesco part 2" / YouTube. Posted
by IonescoEnthusiast, April 24, 2010. [youtube.com/
watch?v=yjRiTGS8n3c] 10/1/18.

"Interview with Ionesco part 3/3" / YouTube. Posted
by IonescoEnthusiast, April 24, 2010. [youtube.com/
watch?v=evev8MJayyM] 10/1/18.

"2000-2007, English, French, Video, Captioned edition: Interview
with Eugène Ionesco" [videorecording] / Radio-Canada.ca.
Trove / National Library of Australia. [trove.nla.gov.au/
work/27340306?q&versionId=46243248] 11/3/18.

MLA Citation: Ionesco, Eugène, Jasmin, Judith, 1916-1972,
Canadian Broadcasting Corporation and Contemporary Arts Media
(Firm) *Interview with Eugène Ionesco.* Contemporary Arts Media
[distributor], Fremantle, W.A, 2000.

EXHIBIT R-7 ▶ 2001

"Ionesco Festival, Production List" / Untitled Theater Company #61.
[untitledtheater.com/Productionlist.html] 11/4/18.

"The Ionesco Festival, a production of Untitled Theater Company
#61; Rhinoceros, Thick-skinned Phenomenon" / Untitled
Theater Company #61. By Karen Lee Ott, Festival Dramaturg.
[untitledtheater.com/Rhinocerosessay.htm] 11/4/18.

"Ionesco Festival, Films" / Untitled Theater Company #61.
[untitledtheater.com/Films.html] 11/4/18.

"Ionesco Festival, Curator's Note" / Eugene Ionesco's Quantum
Theater / Untitled Theater Company #61. By Edward Einhorn.
[untitledtheater.com/Curatorsnote.htm] 11/4/18.

Archives 2001, "Footlights" / *The New York Times.* By Lawrence
Van Gelder, September 5, 2001. [nytimes.com/2001/09/05/theater/
footlights.html] 11/4/18.

EXHIBIT R-8 ▸ 2007

"*Rhinoceros* (play)" / Wikipedia. [en.m.wikipedia.org/wiki/
Rhinoceros_(play)] 11/5/18.

"Rhinoceros" / *Variety.* By David Benedict, October 3, 2007.
[variety.com/2007/legit/reviews/rhinoceros-3-1200555685/amp/]
11/5/18.

EXHIBIT R-9 ▸ 2008

"Big, bold, and unendingly impressive" / Annex Theater.
[baltimoreannextheater.org/] 11/7/18.

"Opening night of Rhinoceros" / *There Were Ten Tigers.* By Sara
Seidman, November 14, 2008. [thereweretentigers.blogspot.com/
2008/11/opening-night-of-rhinoceros.html] 11/7/18.

"Recent Annex Theater Company Videos" / Annex Theater.
[baltimoreannextheater.org/videos/] 11/7/18.

EXHIBIT R-10 ▸ 2009

"'Rinocerii' lui Eugene Ionesco se joacă în Iran" / Realitatea.net.
April 9, 2009. [realitatea.net/rinocerii-lui-eugene-ionesco-se-joaca-
in-iran_492436.html] 1/19/19.

"'Rhinoceros' most popular play of the year in Iran" / Mehr News
Agency. April 3, 2009. [en.mehrnews.com/news/32997/Rhinoceros-
most-popular-play-of-the-year-in-Iran] 1/19/19.

"Aiish to stage 'Rhinoceros' at City Theater Complex" / Payvand
Iran News. September 20, 2008. [payvand.com/news/08/sep/
1237.html] 1/19/19.

"'Rhinoceros' by Eugène Ionesco, Théâtre de la Ville in Paris" / *Les Trois Coups.* By Lorène de Bonnay, May 13, 2011. [lestroiscoups.fr/rhinoceros-deugene-ionesco-theatre-de-la-ville-a-paris/] 11/3/18.

"Rhinocéros by Eugène Ionesco, a man among his ex-peers" / University Musical Society, University of Michigan. By Maxime Foerster, October 1, 2012. [ums.org/2012/10/01/rhinoceros-by-ionesco-a-man-among-his-ex-peers/] 11/3/18.

"Theatre de la Ville, presented by UMS, unleashes Ionesco's 'The Rhinoceros'" / annarbor.com archives. By Jenn McKee, October 7, 2012. [annarbor.com/entertainment/theatre-de-la-ville-presented-by-ums-unleashes-ionescos-the-rhinoceros/] 11/3/18.

Media Advisory, "U.S. Premiere of Théâtre de la Ville-Paris 'Rhinoceros' Kicks Off CAP UCLA 2012-2013 Season Sept. 21-22 at Royce Hall." Contact: Jessica Wolf, August 23, 2012. [cap.ucla.edu/data/press/releases/88_CAP_12-13_Rhinoceros_Sept._21-22.pdf] 11/4/18.

Theater Review, "It's Lonely for the Last Human Left; Ionesco's 'Rhinoceros' at Brooklyn Academy of Music" / *The New York Times.* By Charles Isherwood, October 5, 2012. [nytimes.com/2012/10/06/theater/reviews/ionescos-rhinoceros-at-brooklyn-academy-of-music.html] 11/3/18.

"Early Resistance to Fascism in Eugène Ionesco's Interwar Romanian Journalism" / *Journal of Modern Literature,* Indiana University Press. By Maria Lupas, Spring 2014. [jstor.org/stable/10.2979/jmodelite.37.3.74?seq=1#page_scan_tab_contents] 2/3/19.

Op-Ed Contributor, "The Return of the Rhinoceros" / *The New York Times.* By Valer Popa, March 30, 2018. [nytimes.com/2018/03/30/opinion/rhinoceros-ionesco-iron-guard.html] 2/3/19.

EXHIBIT R-13 ▸ 2016

"Rhinoceros" / Theater Is Easy. By Sydney Arndt, July 23, 2016. [theasy.com/Reviews/2016/R/rhinoceros.php] 11/7/18.

"Rhinoceros" / The Seeing Place Theater. [seeingplacetheater.com/shows/7-rhinoceros.html] 11/7/18.

"Review: The Seeing Place Theater Take On Conformity" / *OnStage Blog.* By Alexa Juno, July 27, 2016. [onstageblog.com/reviews/2016/7/27/review-the-seeing-place-theater-takes-on-conformity] 11/7/18.

EXHIBIT R-14 ▸ 2016

Theater, "In Strawshop's Production of the Ionesco Classic, Trump Is the Rhinoceros" / *The Stranger.* By Rich Smith, September 19, 2016. [thestranger.com/theater/2016/09/19/24568598/in-strawshops-production-of-the-ionesco-classic-trump-is-the-rhinoceros] 2/3/19.

"Rhinoceros" / Brown Paper Tickets. [brownpapertickets.com/event/2586300] 2/4/19.

"BWW Review: Strawberry Theatre Workshop's RHINOCEROS: Funny, but Too On The Nose" / *Broadway World.* By Amelia Reynolds, September 12, 2016. [broadwayworld.com/seattle/article/BWW-Review-Strawberry-Theatre-Workshops-RHINOCEROS-Funny-but-Too-on-the-Nose-20160912] 2/4/19.

EXHIBIT R-15 ▸ 2016–PRESENT

"Trump RINO" / cagle.com. By Dave Grandlund, May 24, 2016. [cagle.com/dave-granlund/2016/05/trump-rino8] 11/18/18.

"The Lesson for Republicans" / Rush Limbaugh. November 8, 2017. [news.iheart.com/featured/rush-limbaugh/content/2017-11-08-the-lesson-for-republicans/] 11/18/18.

"RINO crackdown on conservatives extends south of the border" / *The Daily Haymaker.* By Brant Clifton, September 3, 2018. [dailyhaymaker.com/?p=20892] 11/18/18.

"32 liberal Republicans who should be primaried" / *Liberal Bias.* October 21, 2013. [liberalbias.com/post/2757/32-liberal-republicans-who-should-be-primaried/] 11/18/18.

"OpEd: Donald Trump is Our Rhinoceros; Courage and Truth Will Defeat Him" / *Long Island Press.* By Arnold Dodge, January 26, 2016. [longislandpress.com/2016/01/06/op-ed-donald-trump-is-our-rhinoceros-courage-truth-will-defeat-him/] 11/18/18.

"Donald Trump selflessly volunteers to impregnate female white rhinos for the greater good" / *Ninth St Noise* / "Satire at its worst!" By Dana Worstall, March 21, 2018. [ninthstnoise.com/donald-trump-selflessly-volunteers-to-impregnate-female-white-rhinos-for-the-greater-good/] 11/18/18.

"Jackrabbit Ffeats" / Jackrabbit Ffeats Communication / Michael Jaffe. [jackrabbitffeats.wordpress.com/] 11/18/18.

"Donald Trumpimal Rhinoceros" / Jethro Sleestak Comix. August 30, 2017. [jethrosleestak.com/donald-trumpimals/trumpimal-rhinoceros/] 11/18/18.

EXHIBIT R-16 ▸ 2017

"Yosl Rakover Speaks To God" / New Yiddish Rep. [newyiddishrep.org/Shows.html] 11/9/18.

"The short Version" / New Yiddish Rep. [newyiddishrep.org/MissionStatement.html] 11/9/18.

"Video: Rhinoceros Director Talks Eugene Ionesco's Take on Theatre of the Absurd" / *Broadway World.* [broadwayworld.com/videoplay/VIDEO-RHINOCEROS-Director-Talks-Eugene-Ionescos-Take-on-Theatre-of-the-Absurd-20170817] 11/9/18.

"Review: The Beasts Have Arrived, in a Yiddish 'Rhinoceros'" / *The New York Times.* By Alexis Soloski, September 14, 2017. [nytimes.com/2017/09/14/theater/rhinoceros-ionesco-review.html] 10/9/18.

"Rhinoceros by Eugène Ionesco" / The Catastrophic Theatre. [catastrophictheatre.com/production/rhinoceros/] 11/10/18.

"Rhinoceros Promo" / YouTube. catastrophictheatre, Published on October 31, 2017. [youtube.com/watch?time_continue=74&v=aocanblDhBk] 11/10/18.

"Rhinoceros: Interview with Tamarie and Kyle" / YouTube. catastrophictheatre, Published on November 7, 2017. [youtube.com/watch?time_continue=90&v=aqhS3pSIpFc] 11/10/18.

"*Rhinoceros* thrillingly sounds the alarm bell" / *The Houston Press*. By Jessica Goldman, November 18, 2017. [houstonpress.com/arts/review-rhinoceros-at-the-catastrophic-theatre-9967926] 11/10/18.

"Catastrophic Theatre's production of 'Rhinoceros' resonates" / *The Houston Chronicle*. By Wei-Huan Chen, Published November 21, 2017. [chron.com/entertainment/arts-theater/article/Catastrophic-Theatre-s-production-of-Rhinoceros-12374858.php] 11/10/18.

"*Rhinoceros* Offers an Absurd Take on 'Trump People'"/ *Houstonia*. By Holly Beretto, November 14, 2017. [houstoniamag.com/articles/2017/11/14/rhinoceros-catastrophic-theatre] 11/10/18.

EXHIBIT R-18 ▸ **2018**

[None.]

EXHIBIT R-19 ▸ **2019**

Books, "The Bérenger Plays: The Killer, Rhinocerous [sic], Exit the King, Strolling in the Air" / Alma Books. [almabooks.com/product/berenger-plays-killer-rhinocerous-exit-king-strolling-air/] 1/17/19.

EXHIBIT C-1 ▸ 500 BCE - 2018

"Medical claims for rhino horn: you're better on an aspirin or biting your nails" / Africa Check. September 22, 2012. [africacheck.org/reports/11/26/18-claims-for-rhino-horn-youre-better-on-an-aspirin-or-biting-your-nails/] 11/26/18.

"Why Does a Rhino Horn Cost $300,000? Because Vietnam Thinks It Cures Cancer and Hangovers" / *The Atlantic.* By Gwinn Guildford, May 15, 2013. [theatlantic.com/business/archive/2013/05/why-does-a-rhino-horn-cost-300-000-because-vietnam-thinks-it-cures-cancer-and-hangovers/275881/] 11/26/18.

"Rhino Horn Use: Fact vs. Fiction" / Nature / pbs.org. August 20, 2010. [pbs.org/wnet/nature/rhinoceros-rhino-horn-use-fact-vs-fiction/1178/] 11/26/18.

"The Hard Truth about the Rhino Horn 'Aphrodisiac' Market" / *Scientific American.* By Jeremy Hsu, April 5, 2017. [scientificamerican.com/article/the-hard-truth-about-the-rhino-horn-aphrodisiac-market/] 11/26/18.

"Rhino Horn as Medicine" / Rhinos. By Amelia Meyer, 2012. [rhinosinfo.com/rhino-horn-as-medicine.html] 11/26/18.

"What drives the demand for rhino horns?" / *The Guardian.* By Nicky Reeves, March 3, 2017. [theguardian.com/science/the-h-word/2017/mar/03/what-drives-the-demand-for-rhino-horns] 11/26/18.

"Rhino horn use slammed by Chinese traditional medicinal practitioners" / *The Earth Times.* By Martin Leggett, September 9, 2011. [earthtimes.org/nature/rhino-horn-slammed-chinese-traditional-medicinal-practitioners/1350/] 12/5/18.

"'Cure for cancer' rumour killed off Vietnam's rhinos" / *The Guardian.* By Jonathan Watts, November 25, 2011. [theguardian.com/environment/2011/nov/25/cure-cancer-rhino-horn-vietnam] 12/5/18.

"Javan rhino officially extinct in Vietnam" / *Live Science.* By Douglas Main, January 3, 2013. [livescience.com/25967-vietnam-rhino-extinct.html] 12/5/18.

EXHIBIT C-2 ▸ 2009

[None.]

EXHIBIT C-3 ▸ 2013

"Kenya to microchip every rhino's horn" / *The Telegraph.* By Chris Irvine, October 16, 2013. [telegraph.co.uk/news/worldnews/africaandindianocean/kenya/10384223/Kenya-to-microchip-every-rhinos-horn.html] 11/27/18.

EXHIBIT C-4 ▸ 2015

"How Technology May Help Save the Rhino From Extinction" / *Smithsonian.* By Laura Krantz, November 2015. [smithsonianmag.com/innovation/technology-save-rhino-extinction-180956958/] 11/23/18.

EXHIBIT C-5 ▸ 2017

"Can farming rhinos for their horns save the species?" / News / *The Telegraph.* By Nigel Richardson, November 11, 2017. [telegraph.co.uk/news/2017/11/11/can-farming-rhinos-horns-save-species/] 11/26/18.

EXHIBIT C-6 ▸ 2018

"First test tube rhino embryos could bring extinct species back from dead" / *The Guardian.* By Damian Carrington, July 4, 2018. [theguardian.com/environment/2018/jul/04/first-test-tube-rhino-embryos-could-bring-extinct-species-back-from-dead] 11/26/18.

EXHIBIT C-7 ▸ 2018

"New Chinese Law a 'Death Warrant' for Endangered Rhinos and Tigers" / *EcoWatch*. By Olivia Rosane, October 30, 2018. [ecowatch.com/china-tigers-rhinos-poaching-2616544365.html] 11/26/18.

EXHIBIT C-8 ▸ 2018

"Eight endangered black rhinos die in Kenya national park" / CNN. By Bukola Adebayo, July 13, 2018. [cnn.com/2018/07/13/africa/kenya-probes-black-rhino-deaths/index.html] 11/27/18.

EXHIBIT C-9 ▸ 2018

"Poachers were hunting rhinos. They were attacked by lions instead, game reserve says" / *The Washington Post*. By Deanna Paul and Lindsey Bever, July 6, 2018. [washingtonpost.com/news/animalia/wp/2018/07/05/suspected-poachers-were-looking-for-rhinos-they-found-hungry-lions-instead-game-reserve-owner-says/?utm_term=.bd31adcc0e1d] 11/27/18.

"Kenya poaching stats out" / Save the Rhino. February 27, 2018. [savetherhino.org/africa/kenya/kenya-poaching-stats-out/] 11/23/18.

EXHIBIT C-10 ▸ 2018

"Rhino poop gives villagers in India a conservation incentive" / *Mongabay*. By Moushumi Basu, July 11 2018. [news.mongabay.com/2018/07/rhino-poop-gives-villagers-in-india-a-conservation-incentive/] 11/23/18.

"Greater one-horned rhino" / Save the Rhino. [savetherhino.org/rhino-info/rhino-species/greater-one-horned-rhino/] 12/2/18.

EXHIBIT C-11 ▸ 2018

"North Carolina Zoo Watani Grasslands Reserve" / ZooLex. By Rich Bergl and and Diane Vila, June 18, 2014. [zoolex.org/gallery/show/1188/] 12/1/18.

"North Carolina Zoo Announces Name of Second Rhino Baby Born July 13, 2018" / North Carolina Zoo. [nczoo.org/news/north-carolina-zoo-announces-name-second-rhino-baby-born-july-13-2018] 12/1/18.

"Second rhinoceros born at North Carolina Zoo in 11 Days" / Associated Press. July 13, 2018. [apnews.com/1bc1465366784026a23cff36d1bbc59c] 12/1/18.

EXHIBIT C-12 ▸ 2018

Save the Rhino. [savetherhino.org]

International Rhino Foundation. [rhinos.org]

International Anti-Poaching Foundation. [iapf.org]

Helping Rhinos. [helpingrhinos.org]

Rhino Alliance. [rhinoalliance.org]

Rhino Ark. [rhinoark.org]

For Rangers. [forrangers.org]

THE 1967 ORIGINAL

PARALLELS IN FRANZ KAFKA AND EUGENE IONESCO: A STUDY OF *THE METAMORPHOSIS* AND *RHINOCEROS*

An Honors Thesis Presented to the Faculty of the Department of English, University of Houston, in Partial Fulfillment of the Requirements for the Degree Bachelor of Arts

By Ethan Hirsh

July 1967

PARALLELS IN FRANZ KAFKA AND EUGENE IONESCO:

A STUDY OF THE METAMORPHOSIS AND RHINOCEROS

———————

An Honors Thesis

Presented to

the Faculty of the Department of English

University of Houston

———————

In Partial Fulfillment

of the Requirements for the Degree

Bachelor of Arts

———————

by

Ethan Hirsh

July 1967

PARALLELS IN FRANZ KAFKA AND EUGENE IONESCO:

A STUDY OF THE METAMORPHOSIS AND RHINOCEROS

APPROVED: *James V. Baker*

Marjorie L. McCorquodale

Peter Gruenter

SR Neumann

Dean, College of Arts and Sciences

TABLE OF CONTENTS

CHAPTER I
INTRODUCTION

If one were to select the one writer from twentieth century German literature who had accumulated the most notoriety for innovations of a chilling nature and had also been acknowledged as having more far-reaching effect on later literature than any German-speaking contemporary, the recipient of the nomination would most certainly be Franz Kafka. In twentieth century French literature, specifically drama, Eugene Ionesco would hold a similar position, for he, too, is noted for incredible inventiveness. What his future influence will be, no one can foresee, but the writings of these two men have many overall characteristics in common.

I. STATEMENT OF PURPOSE

The similarity between Kafka and Ionesco is most readily recognizable in two specific works, Kafka's *The Metamorphosis* and Ionesco's *Rhinoceros*. It is the purpose of this study to compare the two works, and thereby to note common themes and devices which appear frequently throughout the writings of both authors. This study is not based on an assumption that Ionesco's philosophy is identical to that of Kafka, nor is it intended to assert that Ionesco attempted to imitate Kafka.

II. VALIDITY OF THE STUDY

Scholarly articles which compare Kafka with other writers have been published in plentiful supply. Among others, the list of compared authors includes Dickens, Dostoevski, Gogol, Hawthorne, and Hemingway. Kafka's universality and timelessness have made him an ideal subject for such comparisons. Ionesco, on the other hand, generally has been compared only with other writers of avant-garde drama. That is natural because of the unique nature of Drama of the Absurd, of which Ionesco is a leader. Kafka is the only non-playwright whose name appears regularly in Ionesco criticism, and in more than one interview Ionesco has acknowledged the influence of Kafka on his work. Yet Kafka is mentioned in such criticism only in passing, and this investigator has seen no comparison of the two authors similar to this one.

Although comparison of a short story and a play is not usual, this study of the story *Metamorphosis* and the play *Rhinoceros* is especially justified for two reasons. First, both works are noted for their devices of human-to-animal transformation. Second, *Rhinoceros* was published as a short story three years prior to its first performance as a play.[1] Both the dramatic quality of *Metamorphosis* and the lively clarity of *Rhinoceros* make them quite compatible.

III. ORGANIZATION OF THE THESIS

The availability of many articles and notes by Ionesco, as well as several interviews of him, is a great aid to understanding his drama. Increased interest in Kafka in the last two decades has produced a large amount of excellent criticism which partly makes up for the lack of essays by Kafka himself. Chapter 2 of this thesis presents several aspects of the philosophies and methods of Kafka and Ionesco to be used as a basis from which to analyze the two works under study. Illustrations are provided from the texts of the works. Chapter 3 is a closer examination of the substance of the two works centering on comparison of the use of physical and mental transformation. The final chapter states conclusions which can be drawn from this study and offers some broad observations on Ionesco's relation to Kafka.

---

1 Richard N. Coe, *Eugene Ionesco* (New York: Grove Press, Inc., 1961), p. 115.

CHAPTER 2
A GENERAL COMPARISON OF
THE METAMORPHOSIS AND *RHINOCEROS*

The two works under study, like any pair of works, can be gone over with an excessively fine-toothed critical comb. Many comparisons of minute details can be drawn, but such observations, even though accurate, are of too slight aesthetic and educational value to be included in a study such as this. Although a quick comparison of prominent features of the two works proves the validity of this undertaking, further investigation reveals many differences in the way the two authors handle a similar situation. Still, important similarities are the main observation.

I. REALITY AND UNREALITY

There are many more similarities between *Metamorphosis* and *Rhinoceros* than just the device of spontaneous retrogressive evolution. Such metamorphosis is certainly the most obvious resemblance, and in both works the audacity of the device creates the same risk. Norman N. Holland warns in his article on *Metamorphosis* that preoccupation with the unrealistic elements can lead the reader to be so dazzled that he sees nothing else that the story contains. The realistic elements, the drama, the characters, and the ideas should all be examined carefully.[2] Ionesco also requires that the reader or viewer notice more than just the bizarre and the unnatural. That is not always easy, for, as Martin Esslin puts it, "the laws of probability as well as those of physics are suspended."[3] One can see on Ionesco's stage a girl with several noses, a corpse steadily growing to huge proportions, and in *Rhinoceros* a man visibly turning into a trumpeting armor-plated beast. Gregor Samsa's transformation into an *ungeheuren Ungeziefer* (monstrous vermin) is no less improbable. Although these unrealistic elements may remain in one's memory the longest, the works of Kafka and Ionesco necessarily utilize such normal elements as characters, settings, and actions.

For example, Richard Schechner analyzed the relation of the realistic and the unrealistic in setting.

> ... Ionesco's settings are always "real" and, as in Kafka, each detail of the nightmare is "realistically" documented. The form—the virtual shape—of reality is left untouched, as are the tiniest details....[4]

In *Rhinoceros* the setting is entirely realistic. In the first act it consists of a sidewalk cafe in a town square, in the second act an office and an apartment, and in the third, a very similar apartment. Except for nonsensical dialogues and droves of stylized rhinoceros heads which are necessary due to the scarcity of well-behaved rhinoceri with acting ability, the world of *Rhinoceros* is recognizably our world. Ionesco's instructions for Act Two, Scene One, for example, tell the reader or director that the scene is a government or private office. Ionesco's floor plan is precise, as are other details.

---

2 Norman N. Holland, "Kafka's 'Metamorphosis': Realism and Unrealism," *Modern Fiction Studies,* IV, 2 (Summer, 1958), p. 143.

3 Martin Esslin, "The Theatre of the Absurd," *Tulane Drama Review,* IV, 4 (May, 1960), p. 3.

4 Richard Schechner, "The Inner and the Outer Reality," *Tulane Drama Review,* VII, 3 (Spring, 1963), p. 188.

... By the left wall, between a door which leads to the staircase and DAISY'S *table, stands another table on which the time sheets are placed, which the employees sign on arrival. The door leading to the staircase is down-stage left. The top steps of the staircase can be seen, the top of a stair-rail and a small landing. In the foreground, a table with two chairs. On the table: printing proofs, an inkwell, pens....*[5]

Quite similarly, the setting of *Metamorphosis* is a totally realistic and detailed middle-class dwelling, the only deviant characteristic of which is the presence of one extraordinarily overgrown insect. Although Kafka does not concentrate at all on description of the Samsas' apartment, a detailed picture of it is presented indirectly in describing the action of the story. For example, near the close of the second section of the work Gregor's surroundings are mentioned in some detail but without great relevance. Staggering in a daze, Gregor had "almost forgotten that the walls were free to him, which in this room were well provided with finely carved pieces of furniture full of knobs and crevices...."[6] In the same paragraph another detail of furniture is mentioned when needed. Gregor's father "was determined to bombard him. He had filled his pockets with fruit from the dish on the sideboard and was now shying apple after apple...."[7] By the end of the story the reader is not at all unfamiliar with the apartment.

In both Kafka and Ionesco the juxtaposed and superimposed qualities of the everyday and the absurd blend to create a portrait of life as each sees it. In *Rhinoceros* Ionesco uses the same technique that enabled Kafka to complete *Metamorphosis* without descending to the well-worn dream-and-awakening device or any other unsatisfactory

---

5 Eugene Ionesco, "Rhinoceros," *Rhinoceros and Other Plays,* trans. Derek Prouse (New York: Grove Press, Inc., 1960), p. 38. Hereinafter this will be referred to as *Rhinoceros.*

6 Franz Kafka, "The Metamorphosis," *Selected Short Stories of Franz Kafka,* ed. and trans. Edwin and Willa Muir (New York: Random House, Inc., 1952), p. 64. Hereinafter this will be referred to as *Metamorphosis.*

7 *Ibid.*

resolution of Gregor's dilemma. The unreal elements are introduced as soon as possible, and from then on are taken for granted. Once the reader accepts the picture of a man converted into a bug, all that follows seems natural, no matter how impossible it is. Ionesco's visualization of a man turning noticeably into a rhinoceros erases any doubt in the mind of the viewer that the characters are really being transformed. In both *Rhinoceros* and *Metamorphosis* there is an early challenge of nature and normalcy—the plague of rhinoceritis and Gregor's shattering awakening—but in neither work does the author ever retreat from that first premise of the unnatural.

II. THE ABSURD

To understand any work of Ionesco requires basic familiarity with the existentialist theory of absurdity, which is the cornerstone of Drama of the Absurd. That theory pictures a fortuitous universe which has no divine foundation, and which provides no meaning or purpose for man's existence. The awareness of such senselessness and absurdity in man's situation gives only an extreme sense of anguish, and that anguish is expressed in all of Ionesco's works.

The word "absurd" is not uncommon in Kafka criticism, for Kafka's writings gave the world a foretaste of the acute sense of absurdity which later writers expressed. Ralph Freedman states that Kafka sought "to reveal man's involvements in an apparently absurd world."[8] Many of the elements which predominate in Drama of the Absurd are developed in Kafka's works, including *Metamorphosis.* Esslin mentions many of these elements, such as the "deep sense of human isolation and of the irremediable character of the human condition."[9] Gregor's hard plated insect form is an expression of his isolation which, once made manifest, becomes more and more absolute. His metamorphosis places him in an irremediable condition which leads to his demise. Another point on which Drama of the Absurd dwells

---

8 Ralph Freedman, "Kafka's Obscurity: The Illusion of Logic in Narrative," *Modern Fiction Studies,* VIII, 1 (Spring, 1962), p. 63.

9 Esslin, *op. cit.,* p. 4.

is the futile and pointless nature of human effort and the impossibility of true communication. Both *Metamorphosis* and *Rhinoceros* present such conditions of man. Gregor's existence becomes pointless, his struggle to retain his identity is futile, and his ability to communicate with others disintegrates throughout the story. Although Berenger's concluding line expresses his resolve to fight to the end for his identity as the last remaining man—"I'm not capitulating!"[10]—every other character in the play accepts the futility of resisting the rhinoceritic wave. Ionesco makes clear the lack of communication through the use of absurd dialogue and meaningless animal trumpetings.

Noting another characteristic for which Kafka is known and which Ionesco develops further, Freedman states what he considers to be "Kafka's pervasive theme: his compulsive concern with the self's insignificance before a world of overwhelming, extra-personal forces."[11] The insurmountable forces are evident in *Metamorphosis*, for Gregor's transformation is without explanation and unchangeable. None of the characters question its reality for a moment. Kafka assures the reader on the very first page, "It was no dream."[12] The unexplained powers simply strike the Samsa household one night while all are asleep. Throughout the story the Samsas cling to "the belief that they had been singled out for a misfortune such as had never happened to any of their relations or acquaintances."[13] The forces or fates they feel operating are also present in Ionesco's works, as Esslin describes. "Above all, everything that happens seems to be beyond rational motivation, happening at random or through the demented caprice of an unaccountable idiot fate."[14] In *Rhinoceros* no explanation of the plague is spelled out, and though the origin of the first beast is much debated, no conclusion is agreed upon. The force which makes people cheerfully turn into bellowing rhinoceroses is likewise not identified.

---

10 *Rhinoceros,* p. 107.

11 Freedman, *loc. cit.*

12 *Metamorphosis,* p. 19.

13 *Ibid.,* p. 68.

14 Esslin, *op. cit.,* p. 3.

Heinz Politzer, an authority on Kafka, gives a very good reason for the force being unidentified, and his explanation, although written about *Metamorphosis,* can apply equally to *Rhinoceros.* "The principal law of the force which caused his metamorphosis is its incomprehensibility. It can only be described by not being depicted at all."[15]

Coe points out that although both Kafka and Ionesco write of a pessimistic universe in which the normal patterns are distorted, there is a difference of emphasis. "For Kafka, the sense of man's inadequacy face to face with the absurd finds release in an overwhelming consciousness of guilt."[16] In his incapacitated state Gregor feels guilt that his family must all work because of his condition. Because of his inadequacy, he "hardly slept at all by night or by day. He was often haunted by the idea that next time the door opened he would take the family's affairs in hand again just as he used to do...."[17] Coe continues: "For Ionesco, the guilt is present likewise, ... even in Berenger; yet in the end, it is outweighed by an emotion still more overwhelming—the consciousness of freedom in itself."[18] However, freedom with logic removed, says Coe, is infinite and therefore beyond man's capacities, causing not joy but anguish. Just before his final burst of resolve Berenger contemplates his position and considers his guiltiness in having assumed that he was always right. After comparing rhinoceroses with photographs of people he turns to a mirror. "They're the good-looking ones. I was wrong! Oh, how I wish I was like them!"[19] Finally presented with a definite choice, Berenger does feel anguish as the result of such vast freedom. "I've only myself to blame; I should have gone with them while there was still time. Now it's too late! Now I'm a monster, just a monster."[20]

---

15 Heinz Politzer, *Franz Kafka: Parable and Paradox* (Ithaca, N.Y.: Cornell University Press, 1962), p. 81.

16 Coe, *op. cit.,* p. 38.

17 *Metamorphosis,* p. 69.

18 Coe, *loc. cit.*

19 *Rhinoceros,* p. 106.

20 *Ibid.,* p. 107.

It is safe to conclude that the idea of an existence not always, if ever, logically justified is the basis of much of the work of Kafka and Ionesco. Both *Metamorphosis* and *Rhinoceros* have that basis, which today is known as the absurd. Freedman says that Kafka's aim was "to show man's eventual dissolution in his world as he constantly sought to clarify its meaning."[21] Gregor succumbs before finding that meaning, and Berenger, though he snaps to at the very last, seems to be left in a hopeless position. Absurdity cannot be clarified in either case.

III. THE BOURGEOIS

Probably more than any other of Kafka's works, *Metamorphosis* contains a great deal about the middle class. Gregor is shown in relation to his family, his occupation, and his superiors. Although Kafka's works express a lot about man's relationship with machines and business and the society which revolves around them, criticism of the bourgeoisie is more conspicuously a constant theme in Ionesco. In fact, Coe writes that "to a greater or lesser degree, all Ionesco's drama is a satire upon the bourgeoisie, its speech, its manners, and its morals...."[22] However, he warns that in Ionesco's usage the words "bourgeois" and "bourgeoisie" go beyond their normal connotations of political and social stratification. Following are Ionesco's own definitions:

> ... My plays were ... perhaps a criticism of the petty bourgeoisie, but the petty bourgeoisie I was thinking of was not a class linked to a certain society, for the petty bourgeois was for me a being who is found in all societies ... ; the petty bourgeois is simply the man of slogans, no longer thinking for himself, but repeating ready-made truths which others have imposed upon him. In short, the petty bourgeois is the man who is directed.[23]

---

21 Freedman, *op. cit.,* p. 64.

22 Coe, *op. cit.* p. 12.

23 Eugene Ionesco, "My Theatre and My Critics" (1960), in "Notes On My Theatre," *Tulane Drama Review,* VII, 3 (Spring, 1963), p. 142.

In another article Ionesco describes the petty bourgeois as "the ubiquitous conformist," the man using language automatically, devoid of inner life and caught up in mechanical existence, becoming indistinguishable from his environment.[24] Examples of these elements of the "petty bourgeois" may be found easily in *Rhinoceros.* Jean places Berenger within the bounds of Ionesco's definition by saying, "You don't exist, my dear Berenger, because you don't think. Start thinking, then you will."[25] The Logician imposes his illogic on the Old Gentleman in the first act, and similarly the office routine of Act Two, Scene One, stamps its conformity and regulation on many characters. Quite near the beginning of the play Berenger complains of the imposed schedule of his life. "I'm not made for the work I'm doing ... every day at the office, eight hours a day—and only three weeks' holiday a year!"[26] He is obviously a "man who is directed."

Ionesco's directions to Act Three indicate more conformity. *It is* BERENGER'S *room, which bears a striking resemblance to that of* JEAN. *Only certain details, one or two extra pieces of furniture, reveal that it is a different room."*[27] Of course, the epitome of conformity is the eventual massing of countless rhinoceri, all alike in appearance, mentality, and sound effects. They are entirely conformist, and undeniably ubiquitous!

It is strikingly fruitful to examine *Metamorphosis* for representations of the bourgeois in the light of Ionesco's definition. Gregor's relation to his job is somewhat similar to Berenger's, in that he, too, complains of the imposed schedule and regulation.

> Oh God, he thought, what an exhausting job I've picked on! Traveling about day in, day out. It's much more irritating work than doing the actual business in the office, and on top of that there's the trouble of constant traveling, of worrying

---

24 Ionesco, "The Tragedy of Language: How an English Primer became my first Play," *Tulane Drama Review,* IV, 3 (March, 1960), p. 13.

25 *Rhinoceros,* p. 19.

26 *Ibid.,* p. 7.

27 *Ibid.,* p. 71.

about train connections, the bed and irregular meals.... The devil take it all! ...[28]

Politzer describes well the scene which shows Gregor as the ultimate in the man directed, and he points out how Kafka uses time to show the rhythm of Gregor's mechanical existence.

> ... The firm did not allow more than ten minutes before sending out after its missing employee. With uncanny and inhuman regularity, reflected in the incessant ticking of the clock, business moves in to reclaim the fugitive.[29]

To be sure, Gregor is not the only character with bourgeois qualities. The chief clerk lives on slogans, slogans which do not always fit together perfectly. For example:

> ... "I hope it's nothing serious. Although on the other hand I must say that we men of business ... very often simply have to ignore any slight indisposition, since business must be attended to." ...[30]

Gregor's mother definitely uses automatic language, especially when she is flustered at the arrival of the chief clerk, at whom she babbles profusely. The inner life of Gregor's father is quite minimal, for he, too, is a man directed, as Kafka points out.

> With a kind of mulishness his father persisted in keeping his uniform on even in the house; ... he slept fully dressed where he sat, as if he were ready for service at any moment and even here only at the beck and call of his superior....[31]

---

28 *Metamorphosis*, p. 20.

29 Politzer, *op. cit.*, p. 66.

30 *Metamorphosis*, p. 29.

31 *Ibid.*, p. 66.

It is obvious that *Metamorphosis* and *Rhinoceros* have treatment of the bourgeois in common. It is also obvious that it is not just the bourgeois backdrop of middle class society and its office or salesman routine that relates the two works. It is the bourgeois mentality, as described by Ionesco, which determines the development of both works.

IV. SITUATION COMEDY

Since both works are developed mainly through presentation of the reaction of the bourgeois mentality to the transformation of others, the works are excellent examples of a technique which critics have noted in both Kafka and Ionesco, the use of situation. R. O. C. Winkler writes:

> The basis of Kafka's method ... lies in the creation of a complex and continually changing dramatic situation subsisting mainly in the relation between the hero and the other characters....[32]

Gregor's situation changes from one page to the next, and every move he makes depends on how all the other characters are reacting to his condition. Even in the very first hour of adjustment to his new genus and species Gregor realizes this.

> ... he was eager to find out what the others, after all their insistence, would say at the sight of him. If they were horrified then the responsibility was no longer his and he could stay quiet. But if they took it calmly, then he had no reason either to be upset, and could really get to the station for the eight-o'clock train if he hurried....[33]

Gregor really longs for others to respond, rather than react, to his situation.

---

32 R. O. C. Winkler, "The Novels," *Kafka: A Collection of Critical Essays*, Ronald Gray, editor (Englewood Cliffs, New Jersey: Prentice-Hall, Inc., 1962), p. 48.

33 *Metamorphosis*, pp. 31-32.

... "Just listen to that," said the chief clerk next door; "he's turning the key." That was a great encouragement to Gregor; but they should all have shouted encouragement to him, his father and mother too: "Go on, Gregor," they should have called out, "keep going, hold on to that key!" ...[34]

Writing of the plays of Ionesco, Donald Watson notices the development of situation throughout his work. "The inflation of the *situation* into the source of dramatic action ... is Ionesco's vital secret. It is the most exciting and the most disturbing aspect of his theatre."[35] Although *Rhinoceros,* due to its different nature, has more plot than most of Ionesco's plays, the situation has as great a role as it does in *Metamorphosis.* The situations of the rhinoceros explosion and of Gregor's transformation are indeed the sources of all excitement, disturbance, and absurdity. Watson describes Ionesco's situations as "perpetual making and unmaking of tension,"[36] and that also well describes situations in Kafka. *Metamorphosis,* as many critics note, is divided by Kafka into three parts, both the first two sections ending with agonizing scenes of Gregor being driven by force into his room. These scenes, especially, cause the rise and fall of tension. In *Rhinoceros* the last three of four curtains fall on tense scenes, achieving nearly the same effect.

Coe's analysis of Ionesco's development of situation is another two-in-one criticism, equally applicable to Kafka and Ionesco. It correlates startlingly to the pattern of *Metamorphosis.*

> Rather than build up a semi-realistic illusion and then shatter it, Ionesco's method is to start with an unrealistic—preferably an impossible, an inconceivable—situation, and then to develop it, still "impossibly" and "inconceivably," as far as it will go, yet at the same time forcing the audience to participate in what is not an "illusion of reality," needing a recurrent and clumsy

---

34 *Ibid.,* p. 34.

35 Donald Watson, "The Plays of Ionesco," *Tulane Drama Review,* III, 1 (October, 1958), p. 53.

36 *Ibid.*

shattering, but indeed *total reality* itself, in all its nightmarish and contradictory absurdity....[37]

The similar transformation themes in the two works require similar uses of situation, and therefore similar approaches to the handling of unreality and absurdity. The predominance of situation in Kafka and Ionesco has led this writer to borrow from the barrenness of television's vocabulary the term "situation comedy." In the works of the two authors under study the situation causes the drama, and it simultaneously creates comedy and tragedy blended together in their views of man in this world.

V. DISSIMILARITIES

Important differences between the two works under examination are not in plentiful enough supply to seriously influence or alter this study. Shades of difference which come to light under close scrutiny will be mentioned in the next chapter when necessary. Although the plots of the two works differ, the dominating situations are alike. The differences in plot detail are obvious. For example, Gregor is transformed before the story opens, while rhinocerization occurs many times during Ionesco's play, sometimes visibly. Gregor is the only character in *Metamorphosis* to change physically, but Berenger is in the exactly negative position of being the only one *not* to metamorphose.

Metamorphosis deals with a small unit, the family, and its reaction to a catastrophe, whereas *Rhinoceros* deals with an unlimited cast of a whole civilization—first a small circle of friends, then an office, then a whole town, including its radio and telephone facilities. Since Ionesco was consciously criticizing Nazism specifically, the plague can be assumed to cover the entire nation. Yet the two works can be interpreted with equal universality. Kafka's concern was not direct didacticism, while Ionesco's was.

Since outward likenesses between the two works far outweigh differences, a more detailed analysis of the main similarity, transformation, needs to be made in order to compare not just plot and method, but meaning.

---

37 Coe, *op. cit.*, pp. 15–16.

CHAPTER 3
A CLOSER EXAMINATION OF METAMORPHOSIS IN KAFKA AND IONESCO

Although the use of metamorphosis in literature is perhaps as old as literature itself, examples of it in works of this century are not many. *Metamorphosis* is no doubt the best known of modern stories of transformation, and *Rhinoceros* will surely live to be the best known of such plays. The actual processes of metamorphosis afford a great opportunity for more precise comparison of the two works.

I. THE PHYSICAL PROCESS OF TRANSFORMATION

The actual physical mutation of characters is an element of unreality, and it is the one element most vital to the development of the physical plots and mental situations of *Metamorphosis* and *Rhinoceros.* In both works the metamorphosis is *down* the evolutionary ladder, from man to some lower rung. Rhinoceri are odd-toed, hoofed vegetarian mammals. The debate in Act One of *Rhinoceros* never settles the question of whether the invading rhinos are Asiatic or African, one-horned or two-horned, but that they are rhinoceri is certain. Being an insect, Gregor is of a much lower phylum and class than the perissodactyles. Politzer has some wise words about Gregor's exact species.

> … Kafka never divulges the kind of insect into which Gregor has been transformed, nor does he specify its form and size…. Whatever vague contours the animal possesses are blurred in

the course of the story by the "dust, fluff and hair and remnants of food" … which have assembled on its back. When the charwoman finally calls him "an old dung beetle" … she does not, as one critic maintains, pronounce an entomological classification, but simply adds an insult to Gregor's fatal injury. By his metamorphosis Gregor Samsa has been turned into an untouchable in the most literal sense of the word.[38]

Kafka's use of the word *Ungeziefer* in the opening sentence of *Metamorphosis* implies only that Gregor is a vermin or noxious insect. All other description of him must be gleaned from the rest of the text. Critics who make an issue of Gregor's exact species seem much like the characters in *Rhinoceros* who suffer from overlogic: "The Asiatic rhinoceros has one horn and the African rhinoceros has two. And vice versa."[39] It is by no means essential to the understanding of the story.

Gregor's basic transformation has already been completed before the story opens, and Kafka makes no effort to explain how or why, since the inexplicability of it is his main point. The opening sentence gives the very moment that Gregor first becomes aware of what has happened.

> As Gregor Samsa awoke one morning from uneasy dreams he found himself transformed in his bed into a gigantic insect.[40]

From the pages that follow it can be collected that Gregor now has a "hard, as it were armor-plated, back," a "dome-like brown belly divided into stiff arched segments," two rows of thin legs of ungiven number, feelers, and strong toothless jaws. His sticky feet enable him to crawl up walls and across the ceiling. One would have to know the width of an average doorway or the height of an average keyhole in a middle-class German apartment of the early part of this century to deduce exactly what Gregor's dimensions are, but he is big enough to

---

38 Politzer, *op. cit.,* p. 81.

39 *Rhinoceros,* p. 32.

40 *Metamorphosis,* p. 19.

move a large armchair, and it takes a moderately-thrown apple to do him permanent harm.

Gregor's metamorphosis continues throughout the story in several ways as he keeps trying to come to grips with his situation. He is astonished by his own voice when he answers his mother.

> ... Gregor had a shock as he heard his own voice answering hers, unmistakably his own voice, it was true, but with a persistent horrible twittering squeak behind it like an undertone, that left the words in their clear shape only for the first moment and then rose up reverberating round them to destroy their sense, so that one could not be sure one had heard them rightly....[41]

For the first half an hour Gregor's voice arouses no suspicion in others since it is muffled by the walls, but by the time the chief clerk arrives it has gotten worse.

> ... They were calling to each other across Gregor's room. "... Go for the doctor, quick. Did you hear how he was speaking?" "That was no human voice," said the chief clerk....[42]

For a long time after that scene Gregor discovers his other changed characteristics and new abilities. His appetite is totally changed, his sensitivities are lessened, and he experiments with his feelers and sticky feet when he needs their services.

Kafka makes clear the degraded state in which Gregor now lives. His locked-up existence creates a stench which is especially offensive to his sister, Grete, who cleans his room.

> ... Hardly was she in the room when she rushed to the window ... and as if she were almost suffocating tore the casements open with hasty fingers, standing then in the open

---

41 *Ibid.,* p. 22.

42 *Ibid.,* p. 32.

draught for a while even in the bitterest cold and drawing deep breaths ... she would certainly have spared him such a disturbance had she found it at all possible to stay in his presence without opening the window.[43]

Gregor is painfully aware of how repulsive he is. Freedman points out how Gregor's condition affects the whole household, even in physical arrangement.

> ... The entire home assumes an atmosphere of degradation.... The three "lodgers" ... typify this oppressive shift in Gregor's former world. An unindividuated "chorus," ... they suggest the intrusion of an entire alien world. They push the family into the kitchen, usurp the dining-room and are treated by Gregor's parents with exaggerated deference. The world has been wrenched out of recognition. For the helplessly observing Gregor, its change has become irrevocable.[44]

Meanwhile, Gregor's change continues. His fatal apple injury leads to his total physical deterioration. When his sister realizes that the creature called Gregor can no longer be tolerated as part of the family, Gregor needs only to consent to his own end.

> ... The decision that he must disappear was one that he held to even more strongly than his sister, if that were possible. In this state of vacant and peaceful meditation he remained until the tower clock struck three in the morning.... Then his head sank to the floor of its own accord and from his nostrils came the last faint flicker of his breath.[45]

Upon later investigation the beetle carcass proves to be flat, dry, and empty, so great is Gregor's decrepitude. His physical transformation

---

43 *Ibid.*, p. 52.

44 Freedman, *op. cit.,* p. 67.

45 *Metamorphosis*, p. 83.

wrenches him from his humanity, victimizes him, and finally forces him from existence altogether.

In *Rhinoceros* the main hero, Berenger, is the only character *not* to be transformed, but since his world changes as greatly as does Gregor's, the required adjustment to the situation is similar. Ionesco's presentation of metamorphosis differs from Kafka's since it is done live on stage, and the exact traits which Ionesco wished to portray by rhinoceri are quite explicit. In Act One two charging rhinos, or perhaps two charges by one rhino, are heard from backstage. The deafening noise of galloping hooves, long trumpetings, and the powerful panting of a heavy beast give an immediate impression of blind destructive ferocity. When a citizen's cat is destroyed by the preliminary invasion no doubt as to the unneighborly nature of the rhinoceros can remain. The cafe proprietor voices the general attitude of resistance, "We're not standing for our cats being run down by rhinoceroses or anything else!"[46] No one suspects at this point that the rhinos might be metamorphosed humans.

In Act Two, Scene One, the origin of the beasts is suddenly brought out. Mrs. Boeuf arrives at her husband's office to explain his absence to his superiors. Mrs. Boeuf has been trailed by a trumpeting rhinoceros which demolishes the office stairs in an attempt to follow her. Suddenly she lets out a cry. "It's my husband. Oh Boeuf, my poor Boeuf, what's happened to you? ... I recognize him, I recognize him!"[47] The rhinoceros-husband replies with tender trumpetings, to which Mrs. Boeuf responds by jumping down from the stair landing and lovingly riding him home. The other characters and the spectators discover that the rising rhinoceros population is due to a plague of rhinoceritis, which transforms people into pachyderms.

In Act Two, Scene Two, the process of transformation is demonstrated. It is the following day and Berenger calls on his fellow office worker Jean at the latter's apartment. One can suspect that Jean is manifesting the incipient stages of rhinoceritis, for his head hurts, especially at the forehead, and his voice becomes increasingly hoarse.

---

46 *Rhinoceros,* p. 37.

47 *Ibid.,* p. 50.

Berenger points out that Jean has a bump on his sore spot, that his skin is becoming more and more greenish and his breathing more and more heavy. Shortly Jean is pacing the room like a caged animal, his skin has turned to leather, and he has begun to shed his clothes. His voice is no longer recognizable but resembles trumpeting. Finally the moment of realization comes to Berenger as he tries to aid his ailing friend. "Calm down, Jean, you're being ridiculous! Oh, your horn's getting longer and longer—you're a rhinoceros! … He's a rhinoceros, he's a rhinoceros!"[48] Berenger runs for help, only to find that the next-door apartment is now occupied by an elderly rhinoceros couple. As he contemplates escaping out the window he makes yet another discovery. "There's a whole herd of them in the street now! An army of rhinoceroses, surging up the avenue…!"[49]

The moment Berenger flees the scene of Jean's metamorphosis, his *own* transformation begins. He is both blessed and cursed by an immunity to the contagious plague, but he undergoes an anguished mental and emotional alteration as he struggles with the humanness within himself. In Act Three he tries to dissuade his colleagues from succumbing to dehumanization, but without success. Just as Gregor is unique in his environment and directs his own end, Berenger remains as the only man and chooses to endure as such in his metamorphosed surroundings.

A comparison of physical characteristics of an insect and a rhinoceros is difficult to make. One important similarity is that both are shielded by thick hard coverings. That is worth noting, since "thick-skinned" today is a synonym for "insensitive." Because of their insensitive and degrading or destructive natures Kafka's insect and Ionesco's rhinoceri have similar effects on the worlds they enter. A wave of rhinoceri is of about the same proportion to a provincial town that a large beetle is to a family of four. There are many ways to interpret the significance of Gregor's insect form. One is that it is very representative of his pre-metamorphosis condition as a petty bourgeois. Communication is nil, isolation total. He is as confined to his new disgusting corporeality

---

48 *Ibid.*, p. 69.

49 *Ibid.*, p. 70.

as he was to his professional position. He is condemned to death by rotting. In a similar way, all of the people who turn into rhinos have rhinocerotic qualities of insensitivity and conformity before they are infected. However, Ionesco chose the rhinoceros for his play for a specific reason, which he stated in an interview for the *New York Times*.

> … Why did I choose to transform my people into rhinoceroses? Because it is the most stupid and the most ferocious animal in the world, and also the ugliest. You saw people change into rhinoceroses in Nazi Germany. They dehumanized themselves and became horrible, destructive beasts in a herd.[50]

Still, many characteristics of the bourgeois situation are used in Ionesco's portrayal of Nazification. For both works the use of metamorphosis enabled the authors to present their ideas with the greatest possible accuracy and freedom.

II. THE MENTAL TRANSFORMATION

Far more important than the physical process of change in *Metamorphosis* and *Rhinoceros* is the accompanying trauma of making mental adjustment to an absurd situation. There is a great deal of similarity in the post-transformational thinking of Gregor and Berenger, for their situations are alike, as Esslin explains.

> … In a sense, Berenger's situation at the end of *Rhinoceros* resembles that of the victim of another metamorphosis, Kafka's Gregor Samsa. Samsa was transformed into a giant bug while the rest of humanity remained normal; Berenger, having become the last human being, is in exactly the same position as Samsa, for now that being a rhinoceros is normal, to be human is a monstrosity.…[51]

---

50 Nan Robertson, "Ionesco Indebted to Kafka and Marx Brothers," *New York Times*, Section Two, January 8, 1961, p. 3.

51 Esslin, *The Theatre of the Absurd* (Garden City, New York: Doubleday and Company, Inc., 1961), p. 127.

The thoughts of both characters are made quite clear throughout their respective works. When Gregor awakes to find himself transformed, his mentality is still unchanged. The reader can understand him perfectly from the start, for, as Holland notes, "for fully the first sixth of the story Gregor goes through exactly the kind of internal monologue any of us might if we had caught a discomforting, but not disabling, cold."[52] Gregor is very conscious of what is happening to him. His first reaction is to deny the reality of his condition with weak optimism.

> ... A slight illness, an attack of giddiness, has kept me from getting up. I'm still lying in bed. But I feel all right again. I'm getting out of bed now. Just give me a moment or two longer! I'm not quite so well as I thought. But I'm all right, really....[53]

As he continually adjusts to his new form he often compares it to his former self.

> ... His wounds must have healed completely, moreover, for he felt no disability, which amazed him and made him reflect how more than a month ago he had cut one finger a little with a knife and had still suffered pain from the wound only the day before yesterday. Am I less sensitive now? he thought....[54]

What degeneration he does observe in himself, such as the hunger for garbage rather than for fresh food, he is powerless to correct.

As Berenger detects that his world is being metamorphosed beyond recognition he tries to be blindly optimistic, like Gregor. He tries to disbelieve Jean's rhinocerotic tendencies. "That's not what you believe fundamentally—I know you too well."[55] Next he examines

---

52 Holland, *op. cit.*, p. 144.

53 *Metamorphosis*, p. 31.

54 *Ibid.*, p. 45.

55 *Rhinoceros*, p. 67.

the transformation more closely. "You wouldn't like to be a rhinoceros yourself, now would you?"[56] Finally he tries to correct the symptoms of transformation—"I'm going to get the doctor! It's absolutely necessary, believe me!"[57]—but they are beyond cure. He must begin to live with the situation.

As Act Three opens Berenger thinks he is observing rhinoceritis in himself, and like Gregor he searches himself for signs.

> ... He puts his hand to his head with an apprehensive air, then moves to the mirror and lifts his bandage.... He heaves a sigh of relief when he sees he has no bump.... He coughs. His cough seems to worry him; he coughs again and listens hard to the sound....[58]

For him the incipient stages of rhinoceritis are purely psychosomatic, a symptom of his unique resistance to the uniforming disease which, in Esslin's words, "not only makes them change into rhinos but actually makes them want to turn themselves into these strong, aggressive, and insensitive pachyderms."[59]

To combat their isolation both Berenger and Gregor long for satisfying companionship. Gregor entertains bold fantasies of caring for his dear sister, and more. He would like to keep her and her music locked up all to himself and to confide in her. "... his sister would be so touched that she would burst into tears, and Gregor would then raise himself to her shoulder and kiss her on the neck..."[60] He clings to hopes of someday rescuing the entire family from their plight. Berenger seeks comfort in his relationship with Daisy. When there is not a single other human in sight, only multitudes of rhinoceri, Berenger feels Daisy's companionship will cure all of his problems. "I

---

56 *Ibid.,* p. 68.

57 *Ibid.,* p. 69.

58 *Ibid.,* p. 71–72.

59 Esslin, *op. cit.,* p. 125.

60 *Metamorphosis,* p. 77.

won't have any more fears now I'm with you."[61] Like Gregor he feels a last-minute wave of hope, a chance to rescue the world—in fact, regenerate the world, just like Adam and Eve—but Daisy, like Grete, doesn't fulfill the dream. She sees no need to save the world.

> After all, perhaps it's we who need saving. Perhaps we're the abnormal ones.... There aren't any more of our kind about anywhere, are there? ... Those are the real people. They look happy.... They were right to do what they did.[62]

To Gregor his sister's verdict that he must go is his death sentence. To Berenger, Daisy's defection to the rhinoceri is the last blow. He is now all on his own.

> ... [*He suddenly snaps out of it.*] Oh well, too bad! I'll take on the whole of them! I'll put up a fight against the lot of them, the whole lot of them! I'm the last man left, and I'm staying that way until the end. I'm not capitulating![63]

Whether or not Berenger finally succumbs as Gregor does, the viewer can never know. Gregor is the first—and presumably the last—of his insect species, whereas Berenger is the last of mankind and therefore has a more historic stand to make. Gregor has never found his own identity, and so cannot lose it. Berenger is forced by his situation to reinforce his human identity as never before. He cannot choose not to be human.

It should not be thought that only Gregor and Berenger have mental transformations, for *every* character in both *Metamorphosis* and *Rhinoceros* is changed. Gregor's family is reactivated when reliance on Gregor will no longer support them, and Grete comes through the experience all ready to blossom forth into womanhood. The three lodgers even take on new meekness and humility. Those in

---

61 *Rhinoceros,* p. 97.

62 *Ibid.,* p. 103.

63 *Ibid.,* p. 107.

Ionesco's cast who are rhinocerized are freed from all moral necessity and can therefore express their innate bestial natures without restraint. The readers and viewers are not exempt from transformation either, of course, since they too must react to the metamorphoses.

The primary way in which *Rhinoceros* differs from Kafka's story is that Ionesco's intention was to portray Nazification as he himself witnessed it. Esslin reports on Ionesco's success, and shows the motives of some of those rhinocerized.

> During the first performance at the Düsseldorf Schauspielhaus, the German audience instantly recognized the arguments used by the characters who feel they must follow the trend as those they themselves had heard, or used, at a time when people in Germany could not resist the lure of Hitler. Some of the characters in the play opt for a pachydermatous existence because they admire brute force and the simplicity that springs from the suppression of overtender humanistic feelings; others do so because one can try to win the rhinos back to humanity only by learning to understand their way of thinking; still others, notably Daisy, simply cannot bear being different from the majority....[64]

Kafka left no written declaration of his intended meaning in *Metamorphosis,* so Kafka criticism has had no base from which to work such as that provided by Ionesco. Many critics have striven to find autobiographical psychology in the story, but most look for ideas of universal importance. Even though *Rhinoceros* is consciously didactic, it is just as necessary and legitimate to search it for universalities.

Perhaps the most important point of *Metamorphosis* and *Rhinoceros* is the statement of the absurdity of the human predicament, illustrated by scenes of man's entanglement in the police state for Ionesco and the business state for Kafka, and demonstrating non-communication and isolation. The works are both beneficially didactic if readers and viewers do all in their power to de-verminize and de-rhinocerize their lives. *Metamorphosis* and *Rhinoceros* are textbooks of humanology.

---

64 Esslin, *op. cit.,* p. 126.

CHAPTER 4
CONCLUSION

There can be no argument as to whether or not Ionesco was influenced by Kafka, for besides statements by critics he himself declared in an interview, "Kafka has certainly influenced me."[65] In another interview, he replied to the question of what has influenced him as follows: "Everything a man reads influences him. But I would name Dostoevski and the Marx Brothers, Franz Kafka and Laurel and Hardy."[66] Still, there is more that relates Kafka and Ionesco than the elements of method, subject matter, and preoccupation that have been covered in this study.

I. CONCLUSIONS REACHED

It is the overall paradox which is presented to the reader and viewer that unites Kafka and Ionesco. Their devices for presenting that paradox are similar in some ways and different in others. Although Ionesco's originality and inventiveness are exceeded by none, Kafka preceded him in the use of unreality, absurdity, the bourgeois, and situation. Politzer explains Kafka's important position in literature.

> ... Franz Kafka's importance derives from the fact that he was probably the first and certainly the most radical writer to

---

65 Schechner, "An Interview With Ionesco," *Tulane Drama Review*, VII, 3 (Spring, 1963), p. 167.

66 Robertson, *loc. cit.*

pronounce the insoluble paradox of human existence by using this paradox as the message of his parables....[67]

All that Kafka did was complete in the first quarter of this century. In
his short career he achieved what Esslin calls "the supreme expression
of the situation of modern man."[68] A whole second quarter century
elapsed before Ionesco seriously took up writing. The situation of
modern man was not different then, but more intensely entangled
than ever. It is interesting that in 1947 Gide's adaptation of Kafka's
novel *The Trial* was staged and helped to mold the Theatre of the
Absurd. Esslin analyzes the importance of the event as follows:

> ... Undoubtedly this performance which brought the dream-
> world of Kafka to a triumphant unfolding on the stage and
> demonstrated the effectiveness of this particular brand of
> fantasy in practical theatrical terms exercised a profound in-
> fluence on the practitioners of the new movement. For here,
> too, they saw the externalization of mental processes, the act-
> ing out of nightmarish dreams by schematized figures in a
> world of torment and absurdity.[69]

The world was becoming ready to see Kafkaesque innovations on the
stage, and Ionesco was becoming ready to help present them.

Ionesco's plays, in the words of Wallace Fowlie, "often give the impression of being autopsies of our unacknowledged, invisible manias."[70]
The viewers of Ionesco's works, like the readers of Kafka's, are presented
with a perturbing picture of their own lives and of their own world, and
they see the vital questions of the age asked but not necessarily answered.

Even today the device of metamorphosis seems somewhat bizarre,
but its appropriateness in Kafka and Ionesco is indisputable. Ionesco

---

67 Politzer, *op. cit.,* p. 22.

68 Esslin, *op. cit.,* p. 253.

69 Esslin, "The Theatre of the Absurd," p. 10.

70 Wallace Fowlie, "New Plays of Ionesco and Genet," *Tulane Drama Review,*
V, 1 (September, 1960), p. 45.

has written that "a creative idea can only be expressed by a means of expression which is suited to it, so much so that idea and means of expression are one and the same."[71] That accounts for his use of rhinoceri to portray those who act like, and *are,* rhinos. Edwin Muir, a foremost translator of Kafka's works, explains the efficiency of transformation in *Metamorphosis* and, by extension, in *Rhinoceros.*

> The mixture of realism and allegory which is Kafka's peculiar invention is accordingly perhaps the most economical and effective means that could have been found for expressing his vision of life.[72]

Freedman points out that the transformations also suggest "the intricate relations in man between a human and an animal nature."[73] In both works the thin line between the human and the animal, if it exists, is hazy, for even the characters to whom it is most important falter when trying to pinpoint it.

Besides being an inevitable and economical expression of man's situation and nature, transformations in Kafka and Ionesco serve a deeper purpose, since the aim of both men is to arrive somehow at the truth. Coe shows the highest significance of the metamorphoses when he says that the use of unreality in Kafka and Ionesco is "a device for attaining a deeper insight into reality itself."[74]

II. CLOSING STATEMENT

To this point, this study has been concerned with comparing Ionesco and Kafka, and especially with noting their similarities. Ionesco is very aware that all writers and dramatists, himself included, are com-

---

71 Ionesco, "The Avant-Garde Theatre," *Tulane Drama Review,* V, 2 (December, 1960), p. 47.

72 Edwin Muir, "Franz Kafka," *Kafka: A Collection of Critical Essays,* Ronald Gray, editor (Englewood Cliffs, New Jersey: Prentice-Hall, Inc., 1962), p. 42.

73 Freedman, *op. cit.,* p. 68.

74 Coe, *op. cit.,* p. 37.

pared continually to all other writers and dramatists, but especially to those who came before. He examined himself in such a manner and wrote the following.

> What is striking first of all … in the new works is the realization that they are clearly different from the preceding works.… Later the differences will become less obvious, and then it is especially the resemblances with earlier works, the awareness of a certain identity and a definite identity which may prevail; everyone will recognize it and everything will end up being integrated with the history of art and of literature.

> … I think it is still too soon to know whether there has been anything new or not.… We don't know, we cannot yet know if we are or are not the craftsmen of a transformation of mentality; we have not yet had sufficient perspective to judge.[75]

Kafka was neither a dramatist nor an existentialist. He and Ionesco most probably were not motivated by the same things, but their works have many parallels. In the light of Ionesco's remarks above, this study should be remade in twenty-five, perhaps fifty, years from now. The two writers may seem more similar or less so at that time, or Kafka may still seem a forerunner of Ionesco.

Esslin sums up what is being expressed in Kafka's and Ionesco's works.

> … Ionesco, like Kafka …, is primarily concerned with trying to communicate his own sense of being, to tell the world what it feels like, what it means for him when he says, "I am" or "I am alive." …[76]

Their sense of being is not pretty, but their "I am" should be significant to the world.

------

75 Ionesco, "Have I Written Anti-theatre?" (1961) in "Notes On My Theatre," *Tulane Drama Review*, VII, 3 (Spring, 1963), p. 157.

76 Esslin, *The Theatre of the Absurd*, p. 105.

BIBLIOGRAPHY

Ackermann, Paul Kurt. "A History of Critical Writing on Franz Kafka," *German Quarterly,* XXIII, 2 (March, 1950), 105–113.

Camus, Albert. "Hope and the Absurd in the Work of Franz Kafka," *The Myth of Sisyphus and Other Essays.* New York: Alfred A. Knopf, Inc., 1955. Pp. 92-102.

Coe, Richard N. *Eugene Ionesco.* New York: Grove Press, Inc., 1961. 120 pp.

Esslin, Martin. *The Theatre of the Absurd.* Garden City, New York: Doubleday and Company, Inc., 1961. 364 pp.

_____. "The Theatre of the Absurd," *Tulane Drama Review,* IV, 4 (May, 1960), 3–15.

Fowlie, Wallace. "New Plays of Ionesco and Genet," *Tulane Drama Review,* V, 1 (September, 1960), 43–48.

Freedman, Ralph. "Kafka's Obscurity: The Illusion of Logic in Narrative," *Modern Fiction Studies,* VIII, 1 (Spring, 1962), 61–74.

Holland, Norman N. "Kafka's 'Metamorphosis': Realism and Unrealism," *Modern Fiction Studies,* IV, 2 (Summer, 1958), 143–150.

Ionesco, Eugene. "Notes On My Theatre," *Tulane Drama Review*, VII, 3 (Spring, 1962), 127–159.

_____. *Notes and Counter Notes*. Trans. Donald Watson. New York: Grove Press, Inc., 1964. 271 pp.

_____. "Rhinoceros," *Rhinoceros and Other Plays*. Trans. Derek Prouse. New York: Grove Press, Inc., 1960. Pp. 1–107.

_____. "The Avant-Garde Theatre," *Tulane Drama Review*, V, 2 (December, 1960), 44–53.

_____. "The Tragedy of Language: How an English Primer became my first Play," *Tulane Drama Review*, IV, 3 (March, 1960), 10–13.

Kafka, Franz. "The Metamorphosis," *Selected Short Stories of Franz Kafka*, Edwin and Willa Muir, editors and translators. New York: Random House, Inc., 1952. Pp. 19–89.

Lewis, Allan. *The Contemporary Theatre: The Significant Playwrights of Our Time*. New York: Crown Publishers, Inc., 1962. 312 pp.

Muir, Edwin. "Franz Kafka," *Kafka: A Collection of Critical Essays*, Ronald Gray, editor. Englewood Cliffs, New Jersey: Prentice-Hall, Inc., 1962. Pp. 33–44.

Politzer, Heinz. *Franz Kafka: Parable and Paradox*. Ithaca, New York: Cornell University Press, 1962. 376 pp.

Robertson, Nan. "Ionesco: Indebted to Kafka and Marx Brothers," *New York Times*, Section Two, January 8, 1961, pp. 1, 3.

Schechner, Richard. "An Interview With Ionesco," *Tulane Drama Review*, VII, 3 (Spring, 1963), 163–168.

_____. "The Inner and the Outer Reality," *Tulane Drama Review*, VII, 3 (Spring, 1963), 187–217.

Seyppel, Joachim H. "The Animal Theme and Totemism in Franz Kafka," *The American Imago,* XIII, 1 (Spring, 1956), 69–93.

Taylor, Alexander. "The Waking: The Theme of Kafka's *Metamorphosis,*" *Studies in Short Fiction,* II, 4 (Summer, 1965), 337–342.

Watson, Donald. "The Plays of Ionesco," *Tulane Drama Review,* III, 1 (October, 1958), 48–53.

Winkler, R. O. C. "The Novels," *Kafka: A Collection of Critical Essays,* Ronald Gray, editor. Englewood Cliffs, New Jersey: Prentice-Hall, Inc., 1962. Pp. 45–51.

APPLAUSE—THE FACULTY

Thinking back to the fertile minds that mentored me during realization of my original thesis, I did a little research on them too. As is often the case after someone we admire has passed, I wish I'd known more of their backgrounds when I was able to converse with them and draw on their immense knowledge and insight. Never take your teachers for granted!

I got to know a lot of faculty growing up, since I frequented the central campus of the University of Houston at an early age. My father—noted concert pianist Albert Hirsh, UH professor of music and artist-in-residence—taught and performed there more than 40 years.

Each with academic achievements that dwarf my own, these were the supportive signers of my original thesis:

> **Dr. James Volant Baker** (Advisor): B.A., M.A., Oxford University; M.A., Ph.D., University of Michigan. Professor of English.

> **Dr. Marjorie Kimball McCorquodale:** B.A., M.A., Rice University; Ph.D., University of Texas. Professor of English.

> **Peter Wolfgang Guenther:** M.A. (and later, Ph.D.), University of Texas. Assistant Professor of Art.

> **Dr. Alfred R. Neumann:** B.A., LL.D. (hon.), Marshall University; M.A., University of Kentucky; M.A., Harvard Uni-

versity; Ph.D., University of Michigan. Professor of German and Dean, College of Arts and Sciences.

All four professors seemed to find my subject matter entertaining enough to actually enjoy the assignment of coaching and accepting this work. I certainly hope so. They deserved a break from their usual routines.

Before Dr. Baker agreed to serve as advisor for my senior honors thesis, he led me through the first of two thought-provoking semesters of literary criticism, inspiring my interest in this comparison of Kafka and Ionesco. I had already read *The Metamorphosis* in two languages, but French existentialism was new territory. Dr. Baker's course ranged from Aristotle to Albee, Kafka to Camus, Sophocles to Sartre. During the first semester it was our analysis of *Rhinoceros* and later *Metamorphosis* that sparked my idea for an independent project, and my senior honors thesis began to germinate. The next semester I continued the course while beginning my thesis research.

A native of Reading, England, Dr. Baker arrived in the United States in 1930. He became a U.S. citizen 30 years later. He had two degrees each from Oxford and Michigan. He was a very dry, very acerbic Brit who at times exhibited signs of absent-minded professorhood. I mostly remember him methodically reading aloud from the endless quotes and notes he had collected for decades—facts, ideas and citations, illuminated by inserts of personal opinion and flashes of sneering sarcasm toward misguided critics or writers of banality. He was not a professor you could feel especially close to, but I did love hearing him hold forth for 150 minutes each week.

I'm pretty sure mine was the first senior honors thesis in which he'd ever been involved. He commented at the end that he was surprised it was such a lot of extra work, for which I again wish to say "Thanks."

The second member of my approval committee was another highly respected UH professor of English, Dr. Marjorie Kimball Mc-

Corquodale. I had no prior contact with her and invited her at the recommendation of Dr. Neumann. She held two degrees from Rice University and a Ph.D. from the University of Texas. I'm sorry to shortchange her mention here, but I've been unable to find much other information about her career. I did learn that she authored numerous published articles and wrote a dissertation on William Faulkner and existentialism. She was also instrumental in startup of the honors program at the University of Houston as a way to compete with other schools in recruiting top students.

When I completed my thesis in 1967, Dresden-born Peter Wolfgang Guenther was an assistant professor of art at UH. He completed his doctorate in German studies at the University of Texas the following year and served as chairman of the UH art department for 13 years. Under his leadership the department expanded both in size and reputation. He also curated numerous exhibits for the university's Blaffer Art Museum and recruited sculpture and art works for permanent display on the UH campus.

Thirty years before he signed my thesis, Peter Guenther was a six-foot-four 17-year-old. He had been brought up to appreciate fine art (his father was an arts critic for a newspaper), so while on a vacation in Munich it was natural that he would want to see the Grosse Deutsche Kunstausstellung (Great German Art Exhibition) at the brand new Haus der Deutschen Kunst. Hitler himself had spoken at the opening ceremony just a few days earlier, eager to boost art glorifying his ordained concept of German ideals. The show was too big to see it all in one visit.

When young Peter visited a second time, he noticed the announcement of another exhibit nearby named Entartete Kunst (Degenerate Art) and decided to see it the following day. He did not realize this second show was not only Nazi-sponsored but specifically designed to show German Modernists and other avant-garde artists, whose paintings and sculptures Der Fuehrer condemned as filth, in the worst possible light. Young people were verboten to attend, but no one questioned Guenther's age at the door. Even though the exhibit was very disturbing, he visited twice.

Years later, Guenther recalled feeling "shock, dismay, and sadness" witnessing the show's derogatory treatment of 650 works confiscated from German museums, works that today are recognized as modern masterpieces. In his essay "Three Days in Munich, July 1937," he describes "hideous hanging and placement, the graffiti-like inscriptions on the walls," saying it was obvious the show was designed "to inflame [viewers] against these works. It was a blatant attempt to discredit everything on view."[1] The reviled degenerate artists included the likes of Picasso, Munch, van Gogh, Klee, Kandinsky and Chagall, plus a host of German expressionists. The show was seen by more than 2 million people, a good percentage of them quietly disregarding the Nazis' critique. His three days in Munich were no doubt a factor in Peter Guenther's one day becoming a passionate authority on German modern art.

A decade after the war, as Germany continued its struggle toward prosperity, Guenther left with his family for the United States. He began his U.S. career in San Antonio, lecturing at the Witte Museum and teaching art history at St. Mary's University. He became a naturalized citizen in 1961.

Having had the privilege of hearing his lively extemporaneous lectures while taking his course Art of the United States, I can fully vouch for the statement in Dr. Guenther's obit that students found him to embody "a perfect mixture of knowledge, charm, wit, and warmth" as he shared his passion for art. He died peacefully on his 85th birthday.

Born in Frankfurt-am-Main, Dr. Alfred R. Neumann was Dean of the College of Arts and Sciences for 14 years, and (*full disclosure*) a long-time family friend as well as my dad's boss's boss. He reviewed my thesis concept, read the completed work and signed his approval as dean. I had previously witnessed his academic side during a semester of German Literature in English Translation, for which he lec-

---

1 Guenther, Peter W., "Three Days in Munich, July 1937." *Degenerate Art: The Fate of the Avant-Garde in Nazi Germany,* edited by Stephanie Barron. Los Angeles County Museum of Art; H. N. Abrams, 1991, pages 33–43.

tured seamlessly, and totally without notes, about works of Goethe, Schiller and many others on up to modern times. Oh—there was also this one story about a guy who woke from uneasy dreams to find himself turned into a—well, you know....

I especially enjoyed seeing the dean on stage at freshman orientation in 1963. He introduced himself as Dr. Alfred Neumann. Acknowledging the snickers that rippled through Ezekiel W. Cullen Auditorium (*Mad Magazine* had a large following in those days), he hastily added, "That's Alfred *R.* Neumann." The remark built an instant connection with his audience, at least those who were actually listening.

Dr. Neumann came to America in 1937 at the age of 16, trained in violin and viola and already speaking four languages. By 1941 he had earned his first two degrees and begun teaching high school French and Latin. After three years in the U.S. Army, he taught German and French at Tulane, then moved on to Harvard and the University of Michigan, teaching German and earning his doctorate in German literature.

Joining the University of Houston faculty in 1953, Dr. Neumann began as an assistant professor of German. After other faculty and staff positions he was named Dean of the College of Arts and Sciences in 1959. He eventually focused on founding a UH campus near NASA's Johnson Space Center. When the new school came into being in 1972, he served as its first chancellor, a post he held for 10 years. By the time he retired and was named Chancellor Emeritus, the University of Houston – Clear Lake City had more than 6,500 students. A short time later he suffered a fatal heart attack at 62.

Today the Clear Lake campus is home to the Alfred R. Neumann Library, which holds more than half a million books as well as archives that include the NASA Johnson Space Center History Collection. The Federal Republic of Germany honored Dr. Neumann's achievements twice, awarding him the Order of Merit in 1964 and the Commander's Cross of the Order of Merit in 1974.

ALSO FROM GREEN MOUNTAIN FARM PRESS

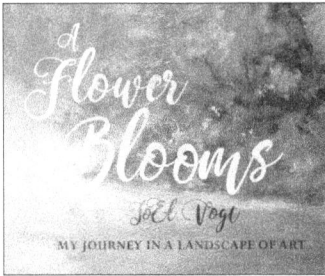

A Flower Blooms: My Journey in a Landscape of Art, by JoEl Vogt

What is the good life? JoEl Vogt has been exploring that question ever since her first childhood discoveries of seemingly vast, untamed land stirred a longing for a wild sanctuary of her own. In this memoir, the painter and art therapist traces her lifelong relationship with nature and her passion for landscape painting. She has contemplated the good life, defined it for herself, and manifested her dream of deep immersion in wildlife and art. Together with her husband, JoEl has created an artist's haven and home in the Missouri Ozarks, where she paints the colorful land and sky.

"The land is like a canvas—not blank, but full of possibilities. New discoveries inspire new ways to connect with the land. The quiet, unhurried pace of living allows time to follow my whims and fantasies. Being here has changed me. The peace of quiet, rainy days, the stirred-up electricity in the air during storms, and the clarity and joy of sunny, cool days, have woven into the fiber of my psyche. In the country, I'm a much more enlivened version of my normal self."

This book is filled with her beautiful paintings of this magical place, as well as insights for defining and pursuing your own dreams.

www.g-m-f.press

www.ingramcontent.com/pod-product-compliance
Lightning Source LLC
Chambersburg PA
CBHW051029030426
42336CB00015B/2780